George Charles Keidel

A Manual of Æsopic Fable Literature

A First Book of Reference for the Period Ending A.D. 1500

George Charles Keidel

A Manual of Æsopic Fable Literature
A First Book of Reference for the Period Ending A.D. 1500

ISBN/EAN: 9783744783477

Printed in Europe, USA, Canada, Australia, Japan

Cover: Foto ©Thomas Meinert / pixelio.de

More available books at **www.hansebooks.com**

Romance and Other Studies

BY

GEORGE C. KEIDEL, Ph. D.,

*Assistant in Romance Languages in the
Johns Hopkins University.*

Number Two:

A MANUAL OF

ÆSOPIC FABLE LITERATURE.

*A First Book of Reference for the Period
Ending A. D. 1500.*

FIRST FASCICULE.

(With Three Facsimiles.)

BALTIMORE:
THE FRIEDENWALD COMPANY,
1896.

A Manual of
Æsopic Fable Literature.

A FIRST BOOK OF REFERENCE FOR THE
PERIOD ENDING A. D. 1500,

BY

GEORGE C. KEIDEL, Ph.D.,

Assistant in Romance Languages in the
Johns Hopkins University.

FIRST FASCICULE.

(With Three Facsimiles.)

CONTENTS.

		PAGE
TITLE PAGE TO THE SERIES		i
TITLE PAGE		iii
CONTENTS		v
PREFATORY NOTE		vi
FACSIMILES		vi

INTRODUCTION.

General Remarks on Fable Literature	vii
Subjects for Investigation	viii
Intrinsic Value of the Æsopic Fable	xi
Mode of Construction and Limitations of the First Fascicule	xii
Non Vidimus	xv
Description of Facsimiles	xvi

GENERAL BIBLIOGRAPHY.

History of Æsopic Fable Literature	1
History of Related Subjects	3
History of Special Fields of Fable Literature	4
Definitions of Fable	6
History of Single Fables	7
Tables of Fable Literature	8

INCUNABULA.

Editions and Descriptions	9
Extant Copies	28
Reference Lists	53
a. Authors	53
b. Cities Where Printed	54
c. Printers	55
d. Size of the Folio Editions	58
e. Size of the Quarto Editions	59
f. Languages	60
g. Cities Where Preserved	61
h. Alphabetical List of Sales and Catalogues	66
i. Chronological List of Sales and Catalogues	69
j. Prices Brought	72
k. Bibliographers' Vidimus	75
l. Former Owners	75

PREFATORY NOTE.

Among the earliest appointments to the Academic Staff of the Johns Hopkins University made by the Board of Trustees was that of Arthur Marshall Elliott on June 5, 1876, to be an Associate in Languages, and it is in commemoration of the twentieth anniversary of this most important event in the history of the Romance Studies of America, representing as it does the beginning of a double decennium of incessant effort to raise the standard of modern linguistic work in the New World, that this first fascicule of a *Manual of Æsopic Fable Literature* is issued by one of his pupils as a tribute and memorial of a long period of labor under his direction and inspiration.

By a singular coincidence this same date of June 5, 1896, marks approximately the close of a decennium of continuous attendance at the Johns Hopkins University by the author of the present book, and at once a lustrum of association with Professor Elliott in his work in Fable Literature, the special subject to which this publication is devoted.

GEORGE C. KEIDEL,
Assistant in Romance Languages.

JOHNS HOPKINS UNIVERSITY,
   June 5, 1896.

iustè eum interfecisse,
etiam cippum erexe-
runt. Sed primates
Graeciæ ac sapientissi-
mi quique, quum &
ipsi, quæ in Æsopum
facta fuissent, intelle-
xissent, & in Delphos
profecti sunt, & cum
illis habita inquisitio-
ne, vltores & ipsi Æso-
pi mortis fuerunt.

Finis Æsopi vitæ à
Maximo Planude con-
scripta.

νι δ' ετι τη εκκλησία εςα-
ζ[...]ντωνε ετι τ' εα-
φαντισαν και αυτοι πο-
λε προ[...]δωντες, τοις εν Δελ-
φοις παρεγένοντο, και
τδι επαρξάντων, εκδίκη-
σιν ποιησάντων, εκδίκη-
ται τω Αισωπε φονε
τε εγένοντο.

Τέλος τ' Αισωπε
βία τως Μαξίμε τ'
Πλανεδε σνγγραφέ-
σης.

ΑΕΣΟ   ΑΙΣΩ

ΑΕΤΟΣ ΚΑΙ ΑΛΩ-
πηξ.
AQVILA ET
Vulpes.

Ετος και Α-
λώπηξ φι-
λίαν ςποιη-
σάμεναι,
πλησίον αλλήλων οι-
κεΐν διέγνωσαν,
βεβαίωσιν φιλίας την
σννήθειαν ποιεμέναι.
και η μεν αναβάσα ε-
πι τι περιύψηλον δέν-
δρον εντεκνοποιήσα-

A Quila
& Vulpes
inita amici
tia, propè
habitare decreuerunt,
amicitiae familiarita-
tē re confirmāres, itaque
Aquila super alta in ar-
bore

ΜΥΘΟΙ
ΑΦΘΟΝΙΟΥ
ΡΗΤΟΡΟΣ.

α. Μῦθος τ̄ τεττίγων ἠ μυρμήκων, ϗ προτρεπ@ εἰς πόνον.

Θέρος ἦν ἀκμὴ ϗ αἱ μ τέττιγ@ εναρμόνιον ἀπεδίδοντο φωνήν· τοῖς μύρμηξιν, ἠ πόνος ἦσαν ἐπιμελὴς καρπῶν, ἐξ ὧν ιμᾶλλον ὅς χειμῶν@ τραφείησαν· ἐφεστῶτ@ δὲ, ϗ τραφῆναι τῇ μύρμηκ@ διὰ τῶν ἐπόνησαν, βέλτιον τῆς ἠδυπαθείας τὰ τῆς ἐνδείας. Οὕτω πόνος ἀεὶ μ ἀθάνατον, ϗ πρὸς ὃ ψηφ@ καταφρονεῖ.

β. Μῦθος τῆ χηνὸς σύγκυκνον, τοὺς αὐτοὺς εἰς λόγους προτρεπ@ αν.

Ἀνὴρ θ ποθ@ χηνά τε ἅμα ϗ κύκνον ἀργύρ@ θρεψεν θεοῦ λόγ@· καὶ ϊ δὲ ἐπὶ

APHTHONII
SOPH. FABVLÆ
IACOBVS KIMEDONICVS
Filius, interpretatus est.

Prima fabula, cicadarum & formicarum, instigans adolescentes ad laborem.

ERat æstatis feruor, & cicadæ quidem cantibus indulgebit assiduis, formicis autem labor are erat curæ, & fructus colligere, vnde hyeme possent ali. Qui cum iam aduenisset, formicæ quidem laboribus suis alebantur, his vero voluptas defiit in inopiam.
Sic inuenimus quandos laterum neminem, in sonschute te est difficili.

2. Fabula Anseris & Cycni; adhortans eosdem ad facundiam.

VIr diues anserem simul alebat & olorum; alebat autem non eodem

INTRODUCTION.

Fable Literature, taking the term in its most general sense, may be said to include all forms of animal tales in which a moral purpose is evident. Such tales appear to have existed at all times and among all peoples, and the attempt to trace mutual relations between them in their oral form appears to be a well-nigh hopeless task. It is only when they definitely appear as literature and are consigned to writing that tangible results in this direction are attainable to the modern scholar.

Fable Literature as a whole may be divided into three main groups: *Bidpai Literature, Æsopic Fables* and *the Animal Epic*. Each of these has its problems, each of these has its charms; but it is with the second of them as lying more especially within the domain of the author's habitual studies that the present *Manual* is exclusively concerned.

Indeed it may well be claimed that in the usual acceptation of the English term, *Fable* refers exclusively to this class of literature, whilst the other two classes (if known at all) are considered merely as cognate branches.

Having thus already greatly restricted the scope of the present work, it will be necessary to explain that even the Æsopic Fable in its entirety has seemed to the author too large a subject for treatment here, and that he has therefore given items of information only for the period extending from the earliest known times of the Æsopic Fable, as manifested in the extant writings of the Greeks, down to the close of the Fifteenth Century, an epoch when manuscript copying as the recognized means of recording man's thoughts gave way to book printing and the general exter-

nal aspect of literature in consequence changed to its
modern form.

The chief aim in the compilation of such a manual has
been to provide scholars with a handy book of first reference which would serve as a general guide to the subject
from whatever side it might happen to be approached.
Its scope, therefore, is quite different from that of the best
work of a similar nature now in the hands of scholars—
Joseph Jacobs' *History of the Æsopic Fable*—its aim being
merely to present the bare facts as far as they are known
to the author, while leaving all constructive reasoning if
not entirely to other writers at least to another occasion.

Should the present *Manual* some day reach completion,
a vast mass of the dry bones of literary history will no
doubt have therein been presented; but, however great it
may have been possible to make such a collection of raw
material, the extent of this field of literature is so immense
that at least as much more will probably still remain to be
gleaned by those that come after. Should any one be
inclined to doubt the approximate truth of this statement,
the author would politely recommend him to inspect M.
Hervieux' immense publication on Latin Fable Literature
alone as evidencing the possibilities of attainment still
open to the investigator in other less cultivated fields of
Mediæval Literature as regards the Æsopic Fable.

In any case it is evident that much, very much, still
remains to be done in this field of literature which was
once so popular with the learned, and which is even yet
familiar in its best specimens to all educated people—for it
would probably be a difficult task indeed to find an intelli-
gent person who had never heard of *the Hare and the Tor-
toise* say, or *the Mouse and the Lion*, or any one of a dozen
of the best-known fables.

Subjects for Investigation.

The general problem in this connection before the
scholar of to-day may be fitly divided into three heads:

discovery, critical editing, and correlation. It is the
author's hope that the present *Manual*, when completed,
may be of some assistance for the first and last of these
categories at least by furnishing the investigator with a
convenient tool to aid him in making new conquests
in the domain of the still unknown. To accomplish this
result his aim has been to compile the pertinent information given by the best authorities on the subject in hand,
and at the same time to add as far as possible new material
derived from his own reading, thus producing on a limited
scale a thesaurus of information concerning the Æsopic
Fable in its period of greatest influence.

It would seem, indeed, that it will be only by gathering
together such scattered bits of information and by making
them generally known that any great advance in such a
difficult field of research will be possible to us, and it is
perhaps not too much to hope that the present *Manual*
may serve as a nucleus for such work and as a starting-
point for a more scientific treatment of the bibliography
of so large a subject.

A few general notions may perhaps be here not inappro-
priately set forth of the work that is still to be done in
Æsopic Fable Literature :

1. A thorough search for new manuscripts containing
collections of fables is yet to be made in the various public
and private libraries, especially of Europe, which no doubt
still contain many treasures of this sort as yet unknown to
the scholarly world.

As an instance of the possibilities in this direction there
may be mentioned the fact that only a few months ago M.
Paul Meyer, the well-known Romance scholar and palæo-
grapher, was able to announce* the discovery of a new
manuscript of the Old French collection of fables written
by Marie de France, perhaps the most talented of all the
Mediæval fabulists. If this is still possible in the case of so

* *Romania*, Vol. XXV (1896), p. 154, note 1.

celebrated an author and for a large public library like the
Bibliothèque Nationale at Paris, what may we not yet hope
to find in the case of less known authors and smaller
libraries? A bibliographical contribution to this side of
Æsopic Fable Literature is included in the proposed plan
for the present *Manual*, though postponed to a later fascicule.

2. With the art of printing as a means of literary propa-
gation came a revival of interest in Æsopic Fable Literature, and for the first century or two after its invention
editions of the various collections then in vogue followed
each other with great rapidity. An individual and also a
comparative study of these editions is surely an important
part of the fable investigator's task, besides offering much
of interest from other points of view.   It is with this aspect
of the subject that the present fascicule is chiefly concerned,
and in spite of the rather formidable array which it has been
so far possible for the author to set up, it seems not unlikely
that the discoveries still to be made in this direction will
be even greater than in the case of the manuscripts, for in
spite of the excellent work done by the numerous and
justly celebrated bibliographers of the present as well as
of the last century, it seems that but a beginning has been
made in this sphere of investigation.

3. Citations of Æsopic fables in illustration of some point
in an author's works have at all times been numerous, and
in addition to this there are to be found many references
to this sort of literature which are of value especially in an
investigation of the earliest phases of its development.
This class of citations and references, while of considerable
importance to fable scholars, is perhaps the most difficult
of all to control.   It would seem that hitherto only a small
portion of them have been collected by the various investi-
gators, and it is therefore hoped to make the present
Manual especially full in this direction.

4. The text of every collection of fables should, of course, be subjected to careful critical editing, and all the special information concerning it should be painstakingly examined and thoroughly sifted by a competent scholar in each case. This has unfortunately been done for only a few of the many extant collections, and is, of course, a sphere of scholarly usefulness falling wholly without the scope of the present work.

5. Each one of the known Æsopic Fable collections should be carefully compared as a whole with its cognate collections in order to ascertain as far as this is possible the relations in which it stands to the latter. This is a species of investigation peculiarly difficult in its very nature, but one which has already received considerable attention because of its psychological allurements, and which may therefore be considered as fairly well worked out by the many celebrated scholars who have expended their critical acumen upon this part of the general field.

6. Lastly, each separate fable should be made the subject of a comparative literary study as an individual entity and its gradual development and endless wanderings from writer to writer and country to country be subjected to careful investigation. Hitherto but few such attempts have been made, and even these are rather incomplete it would seem; as a *sine qua non* for this sort of study it is proposed to include in this *Manual*, as being perhaps its most important feature, a *General Index of Fables* giving under each title as complete a list as possible of the places where it is to be found, together with numerous cross references to the various cognate forms which exist for almost every fable.

Intrinsic Value of the Æsopic Fable.

In addition to all this work which is still to be done on the formal side of a complete study of Æsopic Fable Literature there remains a set of deeper questions regarding the intrinsic value of the Fable both from a moral and from an artistic standpoint, and innumerable minor questions which are more or less closely connected with the more general subjects of inquiry just mentioned also present themselves. But little appears to have been done as yet in this interesting field for study and mature reflection, and much of what has therein been accomplished may no doubt be justly placed to the credit of that enthusiastic fable investigator of the last century, Gotthold Ephraim Lessing.

This writer's philosophical analysis of the true inwardness of the Æsopic Fable may well stand perusal and reperusal, as it clearly shows the essential points which constitute the various species when at their best, while incidentally proving that the vast majority of fabulists have had only the most rudimentary conception of the scope and true purpose of their chosen field of literary endeavor. It clearly appears from this treatment of the subject that our most popular fables embody just these principles, while the great mass of practically unknown fables have remained so because of their failure to include in themselves one or more of the characteristics essential to a lasting success.

MODE OF CONSTRUCTION AND LIMITATIONS OF THE FIRST FASCICULE.

In the compilation of the General Bibliography the aim has been to present a list of the chief contributions to a study of Fable Literature both for the subject as a whole and for the single branch of it treated more in detail in the present *Manual.*

The citations of book titles have been made very full in order that such information might be given in even a limited space as would serve to indicate their general scope to those who may never have had the opportunity of seeing the books themselves. The skeleton citation of book titles so much in vogue seems to the writer a matter to be espe-

cially deplored in this age of scientific exactness, as such
scanty notices are usually tantalizing rather than satisfying,
and more often do they perhaps lead the novice astray than
they actually convey desired information to the veteran.

With the complete list of books on Fable Literature here
cited before him any student may approach the subject for
serious study without great misgivings as to a lack of the
necessary material for general investigations, though of
course hundreds of other books more or less germane to
the subject and more or less important in themselves could
easily have been cited. Text editions as such have been
rigidly excluded from this list for obvious reasons, and
also because they belong rather to other more special portions of the present *Manual.*

It is believed that the various lists given in connection
with the general subject of Fable Incunabula will prove to
be of considerable assistance for a further study of this
subject, as properly speaking no such lists appear to have
been hitherto attempted, for although both Brunet and
Hervieux* have made valuable and extensive contributions
to this field, their work was conceived in quite a different
spirit from that here attempted, which, it may be remarked,
is necessarily based to a considerable extent upon the
results already attained by them.

The *British Museum Catalogue of Printed Books* comes
nearer perhaps to the plan of the lists here given than any
other such publication, but its sphere of action is of course
limited to the specimens contained in a single great library,

---

* M. Hervieux' recently published volume on Odo of Sherington did
not appear in time to be included in the list of his publications given
on pages 1 and 2 of this *Manual*; as no incunabula are, however,
referred to in this new volume, the present fascicule has not thereby been
deprived of any additional information. The complete title of the book
is as follows : *Les Fabulistes Latins depuis le Siècle d' Auguste jusqu'à la
Fin du Moyen Âge.* Tome IV : *Eudes de Cheriton et ses Dérivés.* Paris :
librairie de Firmin-Didot et Cie., 56 Rue Jacob, 1896. 8vo, viii and
482 pp.

and it is at the same time naturally constructed with somewhat different ends in view.

The inclusion of the *Dialogus Creaturarum* commonly attributed to Nicolaus Pergamenus and of two of the *Specula* of Vincentius Bellovacensis in these lists may perhaps be considered by some critics as unnecessary and uncalled for, but in any case it would appear that no particular excuse for their presence is here demanded unless it be the possible plea of supererogatory merit.

In consulting the various bibliographies and books of reference while compiling the lists here given, it has been a matter of much surprise to the author to find that in the vast majority of cases the descriptions given were rather scanty, sometimes even meagre to the last degree ; and he has hence in certain cases attempted to supply the information which was lacking, either by way of implication or by way of conjecture. Had this plan not been followed, the descriptions given would have been in many cases mere skeletons of perhaps a single item, and hence of but little use to any one ; the author, however, does not pretend to be in any sense of the word wiser than his sources, and therefore earnestly recommends all readers to look up for themselves the references given, and thus to use the present *Manual* merely as a guide and not in any way as a possible authority on the subject.

Some slips have undoubtedly been made, especially in the attempt to assign an approximate date to all undated editions, and it is to be hoped that these blemishes will be to a considerable extent corrected by persons able to judge intelligently of such matters.

Peculiarities of orthography occurring in the originals have been kept where known, but the great majority of them have probably been omitted by the various bibliographers whose works have been drawn upon.

Besides the numerous cases in which the descriptions furnished by the bibliographers afford conflicting evidence, the chief matter of regret must remain the fact that it has been their almost universal custom to omit a statement as to whether their material was derived at first hand or not; to obviate this difficulty as much as possible, the statement that an actual inspection of the work in question has been made by the bibliographer cited, is given in a foot-note wherever there appeared to be sufficient justification for so doing.

It has given the author especial pleasure to have been able to point out the existence of several extant copies of Fable Incunabula now preserved in American libraries, as none of them appear to have been known to previous bibliographers. The treasures of this sort still hidden away in the public and private libraries of Europe, and perhaps even of America and other continents, are probably quite considerable as they are of a sort extremely difficult of control through the usual manuals.

Finally, it is hoped that the generous use made of bold-faced type together with the numerous Reference Lists appended, will make the present *Manual* one of easy and rapid reference—an essential characteristic of such a work only too often overlooked by compilers.

Non Vidimus.

The general practice in this *Manual* has been to give only references which have been obtained at first hand. In some cases, however, it has seemed advisable to include a certain number of references obtained merely at second hand, as at the moment a personal inspection of the works cited was impossible, and as by following any other rule there would have arisen inconvenient gaps in some of the lists given.

In order to make the best possible amends for this unavoidable blemish it is my purpose to state here quite distinctly which books I have *not* seen with my own eyes, with the direct implication that all the other books mentioned have been so inspected:

Page 6, Nos. 1, 2, 4, 5, 6;

Page 7, Nos. 8, 9, 10, 13; and No. 2 in the next list;

Page 8, No. 6;

Pages 9 to 28, Nos. 1 to 63 and 65 to 178;

Pages 28 to 53, all the references in the body of the text, except No. 64a.

DESCRIPTION OF FACSIMILES.

It will have been noticed that in the earlier days of the printing-press very large-sized editions were prevailingly issued, a statement which is corroborated by the fact that all of the editions herein cited up to A. D. 1500 are either folios or quartos. Including the present fascicule there are specimen pages of at least two such large-sized editions accessible to the general reader in facsimile, and it has been deemed of interest to likewise insert by way of contrast facsimiles from two small-sized editions of *Æsop's Fables* from the seventeenth century. The latter are given merely as representatives of a style of printing differing widely at once from the earliest and from the latest usage for such works.

1. In his valuable treatise on *Early Illustrated Books,** Mr. Alfred W. Pollard has given a reduced facsimile of a page from one of Antonius Sorg's reprints of the original Ulm edition of Stainhöwel's *Esopus.*† The page chosen contains an illustration representing the situation in the fable entitled: *De Ranis et Ioue,* which is considered by Mr. Pollard to be one of the best illustrations in the whole work. The portion of the Latin text occurring on the same page is quite legible in the facsimile in spite of its reduced size.

---

* *Early Illustrated Books*; a History of the Decoration and Illustration of Books in the 15th and 16th Centuries; by Alfred W. Pollard. London : Kegan Paul, Trench, Trübner (and) Co., Ltd., 1893. 8vo, xvi and 256 pp., with numerous illustrations. See page 52.

† Cf. page 13 of this *Manual,* Nos. 38 and 39; the facsimile was probably taken from the copy No. 39c referred to on page 36.

2. The largest of the three facsimiles herewith given has been taken from a copy which was one of the more valuable books of the large collection bequeathed to the Johns Hopkins University by the late John W. McCoy. The volume is handsomely bound in parchment, but has been erroneously lettered as follows : Æsopi | Fabulæ | Editio | Princeps | Germanicæ | 1483.

Far from being the original German edition of *Æsop's Fables*, our book is merely a reprint of the German text alone of Stainhöwel's Latin and German edition of Ulm about the year 1475.* It can, however, probably claim the distinction of being the oldest edition of the German version issued separately whose date is fixed by the printer's colophon. M. Hervieux has had the good fortune of being able to inspect two other copies of this edition (the only copies hitherto known to exist, it would seem), and according to his description the book is a folio of 169 leaves, of which the *Life of Æsop* and the text of the fables occupy the first 154 leaves, while the remainder contain a work entitled *Historia Sigismunde.*

The McCoy copy is unfortunately not entirely complete, though the lost portions are of no great extent. The first 34 leaves contain the *Life of Æsop* already mentioned and preceded by a full-page portrait headed *Esopus* on the verso of the first leaf. The leaves in this portion of the book are entirely devoid of any numbering. The text is headed as follows :

Vita Esopi fabulatoris clarissimi e greco | latina per Rimicin(m) facta ad reuerendissimu(m) | patrem dominum Anthonium Tituli sancti | Chrisogoni prespiterum Cardinalem.

The entire text, however, is in German, as we find explained further down the page by the words :

. . . ausz latein von doctore heinrico steinho | wel schlecht vn(d) verstentlich geteütscht.

---

* Cf. page 16 of this *Manual*, and the references there given.

Up to this point there appear to be no leaves missing, although the text of the first six has suffered a partial loss at the lower corners, apparently owing to excessive thumbing previous to the time of the present binding.

There then follow 120 numbered leaves containing the text of the fables, but of this series the fifth and sixth leaves are missing. Finally there comes a series of only eight additional unnumbered leaves containing a species of *Index Rerum*, a portion of the *Historia Sigismunde* and the printer's colophon. According to M. Hervieux' description there must therefore be seven more leaves missing from the McCoy copy in this portion. Indeed the verso of the next to last leaf breaks off abruptly thus:

sy inwendigen allein dÿe thür auf vnnd nam alldo—

At the top of the recto of the last leaf there occurs a colophon worded thus:

> Esopus der hochberümbt fabeltichter—mit
> etlichen zuogelegten fabeln Rimicy vund
> Auiani—vnd d' histori sigismunde der toh-
> ter des fürsten Tancredi vnd des iünglin
> ges Gwisgardi enndet sich hie—Gedruckt
> vnd vollendet in der hochwirdigen vnnd
> keiserlichen stat Augspurg—von Antho-
> nio Sorg am montag nach Agathe Da
> man zalt nach Cristi geburt—M—CCCC
> vnd in dem—LXXXIII—Iar—

The remainder of the leaf is blank, and on its verso there is written in pale black ink the name Johannes Schaff-haüsser, probably one of the early owners of this copy.

The present size of the leaves is about seven inches by ten, the type used is the Gothic, and the whole work is adorned by numerous rudely executed wood-cuts. The normal number of lines on full pages appears to be 36, although some have only 35; it is also to be noted that the following leaves are wrongly numbered: leaf xii is given as xiii; leaf liiii has no number; leaf lvi is given as li; leaf xci is given as ci; and leaf cxv is given as cv.

A note in pale black ink on the upper margin of leaf xvi gives evidence of trimming by the binder, who appears to have greatly reduced what was originally a wide margin. The verso of this same leaf has had an extra illustration pasted over the one originally printed in the text, and as the superimposed wood-cut suits the accompanying text yet appears to be wholly different from the one beneath,* though in the same style as the remaining illustrations, we may suppose that the printer erroneously inserted an irrelevant wood-cut in his text at this point, and discovering this fact after the leaf was printed struck off special copies of the proper illustration and thus corrected his original error as well as he could. It would be of interest to note whether the same thing was done in the case of the other two copies mentioned above.

Many of the illustrations have been touched up with either black or red ink, and various marginal notes and other marks are to be found which are evidently due to some one or more of the early possessors of this copy.

A point worthy of note, and one which would probably suffice to easily identify all the extant copies of this edition, is that in certain cases a blank space has been left in the body of the text which should have been filled out by some word not inserted by the printer. Thus among the unnumbered leaves at the beginning of the book there is a blank space in the last line on the verso of the twenty-first leaf, and on the recto of the third numbered leaf there are three such spaces, the first of which has been filled in with a pen, the second crossed out, and the third left blank. It is this last-mentioned page which has been chosen for pre-

---

* This illustration is no doubt the same as the one correctly inserted in the text on the recto of leaf li.

senting in facsimile, as the occurrence of such a series of
blank spaces is perhaps the most curious feature in the
whole book.

The original is about one-fourth larger in its dimensions
than would appear from the facsimile, in which the wide
margin has also been much reduced. As the paper in the
original is rather thin, and as at the same time the ink used
is extremely black, there are noticeable in the facsimile
faint traces of the wood-cut on the verso as well as of the
accompanying text itself.

The wood-cuts used in this edition are probably identical
with those occurring in that from which Mr. Pollard's facsimile was taken, as the one there reproduced also occurs
in the McCoy copy here described.

3. The first of the two smaller facsimiles given repre-
sents very accurately the appearance of the original,
excepting that the whole background is of the mellow tint
which even the whitest of paper assumes with age. The
two pages chosen represent the end of the diffuse *Life of
Æsop*, which occupies almost all of the preceding portion
of the book, and the beginning of the fables themselves.
The original is bound in parchment and formerly contained
two medallions on the outside of the cover, as well as
fastenings of some sort or other. The fly-leaf is occupied
by the following inscription:

Ingeniosissimo puero | Cornelio Luackio | Curatores et
rector | scholae Brielanae* | Hoc industriae | Praemium |
L. M. D. D. | Leonardus Iohannis F. | Theophilus Rycke-
waert | Corn. Bunzolzdt | Franciscus Villeius | rector.

* Briel is a fortified seaport town on the north side of the island of
Voorne, S. Holland, and lying about fourteen miles west of Rotterdam.
From 1585 to 1616 it was held by England as security for certain
advances made to the states of Holland, and it was probably some time
during this period in its history that the award of the present school-
prize occurred.

The title-page reads as follows:

ÆSOPI PHRYGIS

FABVLÆ, ELEGANTIS-
SIMIS ICONIBVS
illustratæ.

CVM LATINA VERSIONE,
Græco textui adiuncta.*

. . . . . .

Adiectæ sunt diuersorum fabulæ, nec non
opuscula quæ in sequenti pagina
videre est.

LVGDVNI,

Sumptibus Ioannis Iullieron.

M. DCIX.

On the reverse side of the title-page there is given a brief table of contents, and then on page 3 there begins the body of the text with: Ex Aphtho- | nij sophistæ præexerci- | tamentis. On the following page we find: Ex Philo- | strati imaginibus | fabula, with an illustration which is curiously enough repeated on page 10.

On page 7 begins: Æsopi Fa- | bulatoris vita, à Ma- | ximo Planude con- | scripta. This portion of the book contains some thirty-four woodcuts. Thereafter come, as shown in the facsimile, the fables themselves, occupying pages 139–305 and numbered consecutively up to 150. This portion of the book contains fifty-two woodcuts.

Up to this point the Greek text and its Latin translation have been arranged throughout in parallel columns on the same page; but from page 306 to page 363 the two texts are arranged on opposite pages, as is also the case from

---

* The next following portion has been partially erased in the copy at hand.

page 366 to page 399, whilst for the rest of the book no parallel texts occur.

Pages 306-333 are occupied by: Gabriæ Græci | Tetrasticha, numbering forty-three fables. Pages 334-363 by: Homeri Ranarum | (et) Murium pugna, after which comes a two-page index of the proper names therein occurring. Four pages are next devoted to a species of preface headed: Aristobulus Apo- | stolicus sacer diaconus iis qui | hoc usuri sunt libro, | S. D.

Pages 370-399 are occupied by a piece entitled: Felium Muriumque | pugna, incerto auctore, followed on page 400 by an index of proper names.

Then come forty-two Latin fables headed: Æsopi Fabulæ XLII | ab Avieno elego | carmine conscriptæ; they are preceded by two short prefaces, and the whole occupies pages 401-427. On page 428 is given a list entitled: Capita Æsopi | Vitae, and this is followed on pages 429-432 by an Index Fabularum, which closes the book.

Another case of a double use being made of the same illustration occurs on pages 169 and 289 for the fables entitled *Mulier et Gallina* and *Gallina auripara* respectively. A number of typographical errors have been noticed, and it is a matter of some surprise to find that the two prefaces on pages 401 and 402, as well as fables 30 to 42 of the Avianus collection, have been put in the same small type in which the indices are given.

4. The last facsimile given is taken from another edition of fables of a later date and of a different scope, but of much the same size and typographical workmanship as that just described, the chief exception being the complete omission of illustrations. The two pages chosen represent the beginning of the fables of Aphthonius, although occurring well on towards the end of the book. The original has been inadequately protected from the rough usage which it has received by an indifferent leather binding apparently contemporaneous with the printing.

On the margin of the title-page there is to be found in writing the legend: Ex libris Dr. Eligii De Longo jumello, a phrase which is repeated on the margin of page 21, thus possibly indicating the birth-year of the original possessor of this copy. The title-page reads as follows:

Α Φ Θ Ο Ν Ι Ο Υ
ΣΟΦΙΣΤΟΥ
Π Ρ Ο Γ Υ Μ Ν Α Σ Μ Α Τ Α.

APHTHONII
SOPHISTÆ
PROGYMNASMATA.

FRANCISCO SCOBARIO *Interprete* : *cum Notis & Commentariis Hadamarij.*

Eiusdem APHTHONII FABVLÆ nunc primùm in lucem prolatæ.

Editio noua à P. S. I. aucta & recognita, & ad vsum studiosæ iuuentutis accommodata.

PARISIIS,
Apud SIMONEM BENARD, viâ Iacobæâ, sub Imagine Divæ Mariæ de Fide, è Regione Collegij Societatis IESV.

M. DC. LXVI.

The reverse of the title-page together with the ten following pages contain a detailed table of contents of very clumsy typographical workmanship, a few almost wholly illegible signatures being given at the bottom of the pages.

There then follow the *Progymnasmata* of Aphthonius with a parallel-page Latin translation by Franciscus Scobarius, the whole occupying pages 1–121. Then at length come the fables, as shown in the facsimile, extending to page 161 and being forty in number.

The majority of the pages up to this point have their
margins partially filled by short printed critical and ex-
planatory notes, and the remaining seventeen pages of the
book arranged in signatures are devoted to a similar set
of longer notes entitled : In Aphthonii | Progymnasmata |
Scholia. | Ab vno è Societ. Iesu Reuer. Patr. | huic Edi-
tioni nunc primùm addita; and : In Aphthonii | Progym-
nasmata, | Notæ ex Comment. Hadamarii. | In Chria. III.
Progymnasmate respectively ; the latter with certain marginal notes in print. Typographical errors are numerous
in this edition as well, and the printing is on the whole not
as satisfactory as that of the earlier edition just described.

1. **Anonymous,** *Essai sur la Fable et sur les Fabulistes
avant La Fontaine.* In : *Œuvres Complètes de La
Fontaine,* avec les notes de tous les commentateurs
et des notices historiques en tête de chaque ou-
vrage. Fables : Tome I; pp. 81–142. Paris, chez
P. Dupont, libraire-éditeur, 1826. 8vo, iv and
393 pp.

2. **Édélestand Du Méril,** *Histoire de la Fable Ésopique.*
In his : *Poésies Inédites du Moyen Âge,* précédées
d'une histoire de la fable ésopique, pp. 1–167.
Paris : librairie Franck, 67 Rue Richelieu, 1854.
8vo, 456 pp.

3. **Léopold Hervieux,** *Les Fabulistes Latins depuis le
Siècle d'Auguste jusqu'à la Fin du Moyen Âge.*
Tome I : *Phèdre et ses Anciens Imitateurs Directs
et Indirects.* Paris : librairie de Firmin-Didot et
Cie., 56 Rue Jacob, 1884. 8vo, viii and 729 pp.
Tome II : *Phèdre et ses Anciens Imitateurs Directs
et Indirects.* Paris : librairie de Firmin-Didot et
Cie., 56 Rue Jacob, 1884. 8vo, 852 pp.
Tome III : *Avianus et ses Anciens Imitateurs.*
Paris : librairie de Firmin-Didot et Cie., 56 Rue
Jacob, 1894. 8vo, iii and 530 pp.
Tome IV* : *Phèdre et ses Anciens Imitateurs
Directs et Indirects.* Tome I, deuxième édition,
entièrement refondue. Paris : librairie de Firmin-
Didot et Cie., 56 Rue Jacob, 1893. 8vo, xii and
834 pp.
Tome V* : *Phèdre et ses Anciens Imitateurs,
Directs et Indirects.* Tome II, deuxième édition,

---

* Thus denominated by me for purposes of compact reference.

entièrement refondue. Paris: librairie de Firmin-Didot et Cie., 56 Rue Jacob, 1894. 8vo, 808 pp.

4. **Joseph Jacobs,** *History of the Æsopic Fable.* In: *The Fables of Æsop,* as first printed by William Caxton in 1484 with those of Avian, Alfonso and Poggio, now again edited and induced by Joseph Jacobs. Vol. I. London: published by David Nutt, in the Strand, 1889. 8vo, xx and 283 pp.

5. **F. Max Müller,** *On the Migration of Fables.* In: *Chips From a German Workshop,* by F. Max Müller. Vol. IV, pp. 145–209. London: Longmans, Green & Co., 1875. 8vo, viii and 581 pp. Also in: *Selected Essays on Language, Mythology and Religion,* by F. Max Müller. Vol. I, pp. 500–576. London: Longmans, Green & Co., 1881. 8vo, viii and 623 pp.

6. **A. C. M. Robert,** *Essai sur les Auteurs dont les Fables ont Précédé Celles de La Fontaine.* In: *Fables Inédites des XIIe, XIIIe et XIVe Siècles, et Fables de La Fontaine,* rapprochées de celles de tous les auteurs qui avoient, avant lui, traité les mêmes sujets, par A. C. M. Robert. Tome I, pp. xiii–ccxlviii. Paris: Étienne Cabin, libraire-éditeur, Rue de La Harpe, No. 50 *bis,* 1825. 8vo, cclxii and 368 pp.

7. **A. Wagener,** *Essai sur les Rapports qui Existent entre les Apologues de l'Inde et les Apologues de la Grèce.* In: *Mémoires Couronnés et Mémoires des Savants Étrangers,* publiés par l'Académie Royale de Sciences, des Lettres et des Beaux-Arts de Belgique. Tome XXV (1851–1853), pp. 1–126 (at the end). Bruxelles, M. Hayez, imprimeur de l'Académie Royale, 1854. 4to, vi and 670 pp. + 41 pl. and 3 maps.

HISTORY OF RELATED SUBJECTS.

1. **Joseph Bédier**, *Les Fabliaux;* études de littérature
populaire et d'histoire littéraire du Moyen Âge.
(*Bibl. Éc. Hautes Études*, Fasc. 98.) Paris: Émile
Bouillon, éditeur, 67 Rue Richelieu, 1893. 8vo,
xxvii and 485 pp. Deuxième édition, revue et
corrigée, 1895. 8vo, viii and 499 pp.

2. **Domenico Comparetti**, *Researches Respecting the
Book of Sindibâd.* London: published for the
Folk-Lore Society by Elliot Stock, 1882. Vol.
IX, 8vo, viii and 167 pp.

3. **Bruno Herlet**, *Beiträge zur Geschichte der Äsopischen
Fabel im Mittelalter.* Programm. Bamberg, W.
Gärtner's Buchdruckerei (D. Siebenkees), 1892.
8vo, 113 pp.

4. **Otto Keller**, *Thiere des Classischen Alterthums in Cul-
turgeschichtlicher Beziehung.* Innsbruck, Verlag
der Wagner'schen Universitäts-Buchhandlung,
1887. 8vo, ix and 448 pp. (Cf. esp. his notes.)

5. **Eduard Kolloff**, *Die Sagenhafte und Symbolische
Thiergeschichte des Mittelalters.* In: *Historisches
Taschenbuch,* herausgegeben von Friedrich von
Raumer. Vierter Folge, achter Jahrgang, pp. 177–
269. Leipzig: F. A. Brockhaus, 1867. 12mo,
vi and 430 pp.

6. **Marcus Landau**, *Die Quellen des Dekameron.* Zweite
sehr vermehrte und verbesserte Auflage. Stuttgart: J. Scheible's Verlagsbuchhandlung, 1884.
8vo, xviii and 345 pp.

7. **Charles Louandre**, *L'Épopée des Animaux.* In:
Revue des Deux Mondes, XXIIIe année, seconde
série de la nouvelle période. Tome IV, pp. 929–
953 and 1126–1152. Paris: Bureau de la Revue
des Deux Mondes, 20 Rue Saint-Benoît, 1853.
8vo, 1272 pp. Ditto, XXIVe année: Tome V, pp.
308–340. Paris, 1854. 8vo, 1280 pp.

8. **C. Prantl,** *Einige Reste des Thier-Epos bei den Sammel-schriftstellern und Naturhistorikern des Späteren Alterthums.* In : *Philologus ;* Zeitschrift für das klassische Alterthum, herausgegeben von F. W. Schneidewin, Vol. VII, pp. 61–76. Göttingen, Verlag der Dieterichschen Buchhandlung, 1852. 8vo, iv and 768 pp.

9. **H. L. D. Ward,** *Catalogue of Romances in the Department of Manuscripts in the British Museum.* Vol. II. Printed by order of the Trustees : sold at the British Museum, 1893.   8vo, xii and 748 pp.
    Pp. 111–271 : *Eastern Legends and Tales.*
    Pp. 368–396 : *Reynard the Fox.*

HISTORY OF SPECIAL FIELDS OF FABLE LITERATURE.

1. **Joseph Bédier,** *Les Contes d'Animaux dans l'Antiquité Gréco-Latine.* In his : *Les Fabliaux,* 1st ed., pp. 64–77 ; 2d ed., pp. 93–106.   (See p. 3.)
2. **Richard Bentley,** *De Aesopo et Aliis Fabularum Scriptoribus.* In : *Ioannis Alberti Fabricii Bibliotheca Graeca.*   Editio Quarta, curante Gottlieb Christophoro Harles.   Vol. I, pp. 618-661.   Hamburgi, apud Carolum Ernestum Bohn, 1790.   4to, xxviii and 888 pp.
3. **B. le B. de Fontenelle,** *De l'Origine des Fables.* In : *Œuvres de Fontenelle,* précédées d'une notice sur sa vie et ses ouvrages.   (Tome IV :) *Mélanges,* pp. 294–310.   Paris : Salmon, libraire-éditeur, 19 Quai des Augustins, 1825.   8vo, 538 pp.
4. **W. K. Grimm,** *Thierfabeln bei den Meistersängern.* In : *Philologische und Historische Abhandlungen der Königlichen Akademie der Wissenschaften zu Berlin.* Aus dem Jahre 1855, pp. 1–27.   Berlin, gedruckt

in der Druckerei der Königlichen Akademie der
Wissenschaften, 1856. 4to, iii and 635 pp. + 24
plates.

5. **Bruno Herlet**, *Studien über die Sogenannten Yzopets*
(*Lyoner Yzopet, Yzopet I und Yzopet II*). Würzburg Diss. Erlangen, Druck der Universitäts-Buch-
druckerei von Junge & Sohn, 1889. 8vo, 94 pp.
(Separatabdruck aus den *Romanischen Forsch-
ungen*, herausgegeben von Karl Vollmöller, Vol.
IV, pp. 219-309. Erlangen, Verlag von Fr. Junge,
1891. 8vo, iv and 550 pp.)

6. **G. E. Lessing**, *Über die Sogenannten Fabeln aus den
Zeiten der Minnesinger*. In: Gotthold Ephraim
Lessing's *Sämmtliche Schriften*, herausgegeben
von Karl Lachmann. Auf's neue durchgesehen
und vermehrt von Wendelin von Maltzahn, Vol.
IX, pp. 7-38; and Vol. X, pp. 329-358. Leipzig,
G. J. Göschen'sche Verlagshandlung, 1853-1857,
12 vols., 8vo.

7. **G. E. Lessing**, *Romulus und Rimicius*, ed. Maltzahn,
Vol. IX, pp. 39-64.

8. **G. E. Lessing**, *Zur Geschichte der Æsopischen Fabel*,
ed. Maltzahn, Vol. XI, 1, pp. 237-251; cf. also
Vol. I, pp. 129-198; Vol. V, pp. 395-460; and
Vol. XI, 1, pp. 117-132.

9. **Gaston Paris**, *Manuel d'Ancien Français: La Littérature Française au Moyen Âge (XIe-XIVe
Siècle)*. Paris: librairie Hachette et Cie., 79 Boule-
vard Saint-Germain, 1888. 8vo, vii and 292 pp.
Pp. 117-123 (§§79-84): *Fable Ésopique et Roman
de Renard*.
Ditto: Deuxième édition, revue, corrigée, augmentée et accompagnée d'un Tableau Chronolo-
gique, 1890. 8vo, xii and 316 pp. Reference
unchanged.

10. **K. L. Roth**, *Die Mittelalterlichen Sammlungen Latein-
ischer Thierfabeln*. In: *Philologus; Zeitschrift für*

das klassische Alterthum, herausgegeben von F. W. Schneidewin. Vol. I, pp. 523–546. Stolberg, O. Kleinecke's Buchhandlung, 1846. 8vo, vi and 769 pp.

11. **K. L. Roth,** *Die Æsopische Fabel in Asien.* In: *Philologus,* do. Vol. VIII, pp. 130–141. Göttingen, Verlag der Dieterichschen Buchhandlung, 1853. 8vo, iv and 764 pp.

12. **Karl Simrock,** *Aesops Leben und Fabeln, nebst den ihm Zugeschriebenen Alten Fabeln und den Fabeln des Remicius und Avianus.* In: *Die Deutschen Volksbücher,* gesammelt und in ihrer ursprünglichen Echtheit wiederhergestellt von Karl Simrock. Dreizehnter Band, pp. 155–371. Frankfurt a. M.: Christian Winter, 1867. 16mo, xvi and 524 pp.

13. **H. L. D. Ward,** *Catalogue of Romances in the Department of Manuscripts in the British Museum.* Vol. II. Printed by order of the Trustees: sold at the British Museum, 1893. 8vo, xii and 748 pp. Pp. 272–367: *Æsopic Fables.*

DEFINITIONS OF FABLE.*

1. **Anonymous,** *Critische Briefe,* Zürich, 1746, p. 168.
2. **Aphthonius,** in *Æsopi Phrygis Vita et Fabellae,* ed. Froben. Basel, 1517, p. 254.
3. **Aristotle,** *Rhetor.,* 2. 20.
4. **Batteux,** *Principes de Littérature,* Vol. 2, Pt. 1, p. 5.
5. **Breitinger,** *Die Critische Dichtkunst,* p. 194.
6. **De la Motte,** *Discours sur la Fable* (*ap.* Du Méril, p. 6, note 2).
7. **Du Méril,** *Poés. Inéd.,* p. 6.

---

* Compare especially G. E. Lessing's treatment of this question in Vol. V, 395–460, as quoted above on p. 5, whence most of these references were obtained.

8. **Eustathius,** in Putsch, *Gram. Lat. Auct. Antiqui,* col. 1329.
9. **G. C. Lewis,** *Philol. Museum,* Vol. I (1832), p. 280.
10. **Priscian,** in Putsch, *Gram. Lat. Auct. Antiqui,* col. 1329.
11. **Suidas,** *s. v.* mythos.
12. **Webster,** *International Dictionary, s. v.* fable, and apologue.
13. **Wolfius,** *Philosophiae Practicae Universalis Pars Posterior,* §§302–323.

HISTORY OF SINGLE FABLES.

1. **Ass' Heart:**
   George C. Keidel, *Die Eselherz- (Hirschherz-, Eberherz-) Fabel.* In: *Zeitschrift für Vergleichende Litteraturgeschichte,* herausgegeben von Dr. Max Koch. N. F., Bd. VII, pp. 264–267. Weimar und Berlin, Verlag von Emil Felber, 1894. 8vo, iv and 492 pp.
2. **Caliph and Poor Man:**
   P. Ristelhuber, *Une Fable de Florian;* étude de littérature comparée. Paris: Baur, 1882. 8vo, 40 pp.
3. **Daw in Peacock's Feathers:**
   Max Fuchs, *Die Fabel von der Krähe die sich mit Fremden Federn Schmückt,* betrachtet in ihren verschiedenen Gestaltungen in der abendländischen Litteratur. Berlin, Schade. 8vo, 46 pp. (Berlin diss.)
4. **Mouse-Maiden:**
   Anonymous, *The History of a Fable;* an episode from the history of literature. In: *Harper's New Monthly Magazine,* Vol. XXII, pp. 240–246. New York: Harper & Bros., publishers, Franklin Square, 1861. 8vo, viii and 864 pp.

5. **Three Wishes:**
   Joseph Bédier, *Les Quatre Souhaits Saint-Martin.*
   In his: *Les Fabliaux*, 1st ed., pp. 177–193; 2d
   ed., pp. 212–228. (See p. 3.)
6. **Woman of Ephesus:**
   Eduard Grisebach, *Die Wanderung der Novelle von
   der Treulosen Wittwe durch die Weltlitteratur.*
   Zweite mit einem Anhang vermehrte Ausgabe.
   Berlin: Lehmann, 1889. 4to, 151 pp.

TABLES OF FABLE LITERATURE.

1. **Table of Fable Literature:**
   F. Max Müller, *Chips from a German Workshop,*
   Vol. IV, p. 171. (See p. 2.)
2. **Table of Fable Literature:**
   J. Jacobs, *History of the Æsopic Fable*, opp. p. 1.
   (See p. 2.)
3. **Table of Mediaeval Latin Fable Literature:**
   K. L. Roth, in *Philologus*, Vol. I, p. 545. (See p. 5.)
4. **Table of Syntipas Literature:**
   M. Landau, *Die Quellen des Dekameron*, opp. p. 340.
   (See p. 3.)
5. **Table of Bidpai Literature:**
   M. Landau, *Die Quellen des Dekameron*, opp. p. 18.
6. **Table of Bidpai Literature:**
   J. Jacobs, in: *The Earliest English Version of
   the Fables of Bidpai,* "The Morall Philosophie
   of Doni" by Sir Thomas North, whilom of
   Peterhouse, Cambridge. Now again edited and
   induced by Joseph Jacobs, late of St. John's
   College, Cambridge. London: published by
   David Nutt, in the Strand, 1888. 8vo, lxxx and
   258 pp. Table opp. p. lxxx.

7. **Table of Bidpai Literature:**
   J. Bédier, *Les Fabliaux,* 1st ed., opp. p. 54; 2d ed.,
   opp. p. 82. (See p. 3.)
8. **Table of Les Souhaits Saint-Martin:**
   J. Bédier, *Les Fabliaux,* 1st ed., opp. p. 186; 2d ed.,
   opp. p. 220.

INCUNABULA.

1. (1461) **Ulrich Boner,** *Edelstein,* Bamberg, Albert
   Pfister, fo. ed. of 88 leaves. (*German:* see Brunet,
   Vol. I, cols. 1096–1097.)*
2. (ab. 1462) **Ulrich Boner,** *Edelstein,* Bamberg (?), Albert Pfister (?), fo. ed. of 77 leaves. (*German:* see
   Brunet, Vol. I, col. 1097.)
3. (ab. 1470) **Laurentius Valla,** *Facecie Morales,* Neth-
   erlands (?), Ludovicus Pontanus (?), 4to ed. of 24
   leaves. (*Latin:* see Brunet, *Suppl.,* Vol. II, col.
   835; *B. M. Æsop,* col. 11.)†

---

*The work cited thus is: *Manuel du Libraire et de l'Amateur de
Livres,* par Jacques-Charles Brunet. Cinquième édition originale
entièrement refondue et augmentée d'un tiers par l'auteur. Paris :
librairie de Firmin-Didot Frères, Fils et Cie., imprimeurs de l'Institut,
56 Rue Jacob.
  Tome I : 1860, 8vo, xlvii pp. and 1904 cols.
  Tome II : 1861, 8vo, iv pp. and 1848 cols.
  Tome III : 1862, 8vo, iv pp. and 1984 cols.
  Tome IV : 1863, 8vo, iv pp. and 1478 cols.
  Tome V : 1864, 8vo, iv pp. and 1800 cols.
  Tome VI : 1865, 8vo, lxiv pp. and 1878 cols.
Supplément, par MM. P. Deschamps et G. Brunet. Paris : librairie
de Firmin-Didot et Cie., imprimeurs de l'Institut, 56 Rue Jacob.
  Tome I : 1878, 8vo, xv pp. and 1138 cols.
  Tome II : 1880, 8vo, iv pp. and 1226 cols.

† The pamphlet cited thus is: *British Museum Catalogue of Printed
Books: Æsop.* London : printed by William Clowes & Sons, Limited,
Stamford Street and Charing Cross, 1883. 4to, 19 pp.

4. (ab. 1470) **Vincentius Bellovacensis,** *Speculum
Doctrinale,* Argentorati,* Johannes Mentellin, fo.
ed. of 400 leaves. (*Latin:* see Herv., 1. 392; 4.
446.)

5. (ab. 1470) **Vincentius Bellovacensis,** *Speculum
Historiale,* Argentorati, Johannes Mentellin, Tomus I, fo. ed. of 155 leaves. (*Latin:* see Herv., 1.
393; 4. 447.)

6. (ab. 1471) **Omnibonus Leonicenus,** *Æsopus,* Venetiis (?), Christophorus Valdarfer (?), 4to ed. of 42
leaves. (*Latin:* see Brunet, Vol. I, cols. 89–90;
B. M. Æsop, col. 11.)

7. (ab. 1472) **Remicius Aretinus,** Augustae, fo. ed.
(*Latin:* see Brunet, *Suppl.,* Vol. I, col. 12.)

8. (1473) **Gualterus Anglicus,** *Esopus Moralisatus,*
Rome, Ioannes Philippi, 4to ed. (*Latin:* see
Herv., 1. 542; 4. 603; Brunet, Vol. I, col. 88.)

9. (ab. 1473) **Vincentius Bellovacensis,** *Speculum
Doctrinale,* Argentinae, Iohannes Mentellin, fo. ed.
of 400 leaves. (*Latin:* see Herv., 1. 393; 4. 446;
Brunet, Vol. V, col. 1253; Brunet, *Suppl.,* Vol. II,
col. 901.)†

10. (bef. 1474) **Vincentius Bellovacensis,** *Speculum
Historiale,* Argentinae, Iohannes Mentellin, Tomus

---

* Latin names of cities referred to frequently are :
   1. Argentoratum or Argentina—for Strasbourg.
   2. Augusta—for Augsburg.
   3. Brixia—for Brescia.
   4. Colonia—for Cologne.
   5. Daventria—for Deventer (Holland).
   6. Lugdunum—for Lyons.
   7. Mediolanum—for Milan.
   8. Mons Regalis—for Mondovi (Italy).
   9. Mutina—for Modena.
   10. Tusculanum Lacus Benaci—for Toscolano (Italy).
   11. Venetiae—for Venice.
† Says at Cologne in the convent of Weidenbach.

I, fo. ed. of 168 leaves. (*Latin:* see Herv., 1. 394–395; 4. 448 and 454; Brunet, Vol. V, col. 1253; Brunet, *Suppl.*, Vol. II, col. 901.)

11. (1474) **Bonus Accursius,** Mediolani, Antonius Zarotus, 4to ed. of 50 leaves. (*Latin:* see Brunet, Vol. I, col. 90; *B. M. Æsop,* cols. 4 and 11.)

12. (1474) **Vincentius Bellovacensis,** *Speculum Historiale,* Monast. Sanctae Afrae (Augustae), Anthonius Sorg (?), Tomus I, fo. ed. of 326 leaves. (*Latin:* see Herv., 1. 395–396; 4. 449; Brunet, Vol. V, col. 1256.)*

13. (1474) **Vincentius Bellovacensis,** *Speculum Historiale,* Parisiis, fo. ed. (*Latin:* see Herv., 1. 396; 4. 450; Brunet, Vol. V, col. 1256.)

14. (ab. 1474) **Gualterus Anglicus** (?), *Esopus Moralisatus* (?), Coloniae (?), Guldenschaf (?), 4to ed. of 62 leaves. (*Latin:* see Brunet, Vol. I, col. 89.)

15. (1475) **Gualterus Anglicus,** *Esopus Moralisatus,* Rome, Wendellinus de Willa, 4to ed. of 20 leaves. (*Latin:* see Herv., 1. 542; 4. 603; Brunet, Vol. I, col. 88.)

16. (ab. 1475) **Avianus,** Ulmae, Johannes Zainer, fo. ed. (*Latin and German:* see Brunet, Vol. I, col. 585.)†

17. (ab. 1475) **Hainricus Stainhöwel,** Vlm, Johannes Zeiner, fo. ed. of 288 leaves. (*Latin and German:* see Herv., 1. 312–322; 4. 349–360; Brunet, Vol. I, cols. 101‡ and 585.)

18. (ab. 1475) **Gualterus Anglicus** (?), *Esopus Moralisatus* (?), 4to ed. of 63 leaves. (*Latin:* see Brunet, Vol. I, cols. 88–89.)

---

* Says 336 leaves.

† This is probably merely a fragment of the celebrated collection of Stainhöwel as first published in the edition described immediately after this one, and not a separate edition as has been supposed by some bibliographers.

‡ Says 275 leaves; see also the preceding description in this list.

19. (1476) **Bonus Accursius,** Mediolani, Zarotus, 4to ed. of 55 leaves. (*Latin :* see Brunet, Vol. I, col. 90; *B. M. Æsop*, col. 11.)

20. (1476) **Gualterus Anglicus,** *Esopus Moralisatus,* Monte Regali, Dominicus de Vivaldis et Filii, fo. ed. (*Latin:* see Herv., 1. 542-543 ; 4. 603-604 ; Brunet, Vol. I, col. 89.)

21. (ab. 1476) **Bonus Accursius,** Romae (?), Bartholomaeus Guldinbeck (?), 4to ed. of 66 leaves. (*Latin :* see Brunet, Vol. I, col. 90; *B. M. Æsop*, col. 11.)

22. (ab. 1476) **Gualterus Anglicus** (?), *Esopus Moralisatus* (?), Mediolani (?), 4to ed. of 19 leaves. (*Latin :* see Brunet, Vol. I, col. 89.)

23. (1478) **Accio Zuccho,** *Libellus Zucharinus,* 4to ed. (*Latin and Italian :* see Brunet, Vol. I, col. 97.)

24. (ab. 1478) **Laurentius Valla,** *Facetie Morales,* 4to ed. (*Latin :* see *B. M. Æsop*, col. 11.)

25. (1479) **Accio Zuccho,** *Libellus Zucharinus,* Veronae, Gioanni Aluise, 4to ed. of 120 leaves. (*Latin and Italian :* see Herv., 1. 438 and 564-565 ; 4. 482 and 651-653; Brunet, Vol. I, col. 97;* *B. M. Æsop*, col. 9.)

26. (1479) **Bonus Accursius,** Mediolani, Philippus Lavagnia, 4to ed. of 50 leaves. (*Latin :* see Brunet, Vol. I, col. 90; *B. M. Æsop*, col. 11.)

27. (1479) **Gualterus Anglicus,** *Esopus Moralisatus,* in Tusculano Lacu Benaci, Gabrielis Petri, 4to ed. (*Latin:* see Herv., 1. 543 ; 4. 604 ; Brunet, Vol. I, col. 88.)

28. (1479) **Gualterus Anglicus,** *Esopus Moralisatus,* Argentinae, Martinus Flachen, 4to ed. (*Latin :* see Herv., 1. 543 ; 4. 604.)

29. (1479) **Jehan de Vignay,** *Miroir Historial,* Lyon, Bartholomieu Buyer, 4to ed. (*French :* see Herv., 1. 401 ; 4. 455.)

---

* Says 160 leaves.

30. (bef. 1480) **Julien Macho,** Lyon (?), Nicolas Philippi
    et Marc Reinhardi (?), fo. ed. of 72 leaves.
    (*French:* see Herv., 1. 365–367 ; 4. 403–406.)*
31. (1480) **Bonus Accursius,** Mediolani, Philippus La-
    uagnia, 4to ed. of 50 leaves. (*Latin:* see Brunet,
    Vol. I, col. 90; *B. M. Æsop,* col. 12.)
32. (1480) **Franciscus Philelphus,** Venetiis, M. C., 4to
    ed. of 24 leaves. (*Latin:* see Brunet, Vol. IV, col.
    603.)
33. (1480) **Gualterus Anglicus,** *Esopus Moralisatus,*
    Lugduni, Johannes Fabri, 4to ed. of 286 leaves.
    (*Latin:* see Herv., 1. 447–448, 543–544 and 547 ;
    4. 492, 607 and 608–609.)†
34. (1480) **Julien Macho,** Lyon, Nicolas Phillipi et Marc
    Reinhardi, fo. ed. of 146 leaves. (*French:* see
    Herv., 4. 406–407.)
35. (1480) **Nicolaus Pergamenus,** *Dyalogus Creatu-
    rarum,* Goudae, Gerardus Leeu, fo. ed. of 103
    leaves. (*Latin:* see Herv., 1. 340 and 375 ; 4. 377
    and 418; Brunet, Vol. II, cols. 674 and 676.)
36. (ab. 1480) **Accio Zuccho,** *Libellus Zucharinus,* 4to ed.
    (*Latin and Italian:* see Herv., 1. 566; Brunet, Vol.
    I, col. 97.)
37. (ab. 1480) **Bonus Accursius,** Mediolani (?), 4to ed.
    of 167 leaves. (*Greek and Latin:* see Brunet, Vol.
    I, col. 83; *B. M. Æsop,* col. 4.)
38. (ab. 1480) **Hainricus Stainhöwel,** Augustae(?), An-
    tonius Sorg (?), fo. ed. of 129 leaves. (*Latin:* see
    Herv., 1, 323; 4. 360–361 ; Brunet, Vol. I, col. 90.)‡
39. (ab. 1480) **Hainricus Stainhöwel,** Augustae (?), An-
    tonius Sorg (?), fo. ed. of 129 leaves. (*Latin:* see

* In his first volume Hervieux attributed it to the year 1482 (which
see) and to the printers Mathis Husz and Jehan Schabeller.
† In both the direct references in his fourth volume Hervieux gives
the date as 1490, which see.
‡ Says 130 leaves.

Herv., 1. 323–327 ; 4. 361–365 ; Brunet, Vol. I, col.
90 ; *B. M. Æsop,* col. 12.)

40. (ab. 1480) **Hainricus Stainhöwel,** Augustae (?), Antonius Sorg (?), fo. ed. of 158 leaves. (*German :*
see Herv., 1. 354–355 ; 4. 391–392 ; Brunet, Vol. I,
col. 101.)

41. (ab. 1480) **Hainricus Stainhöwel,** Augustae (?), Antonius Sorg (?), fo. ed. of 190 leaves. (*German :*
see Brunet, Vol. I, col. 100.)

42. (ab. 1480) **Hainricus Stainhöwel,** Augustae (?), Antonius Sorg (?), fo. ed. of 170 leaves. (*German :*
see Herv., 1. 355 ; 4. 392–393 ; Brunet, Vol. I, col.
100.)

43. (ab. 1480) **Hainricus Stainhöwel,** Augustae (?), Antonius Sorg (?), fo. ed. of 115 leaves. (*German :*
see Herv., 1. 355–357 ; 4. 393–394 ; Brunet, Vol.
I, col. 100.)

44. (ab. 1480) **Heinricus Stainhöwel,** Augustae (?),
Guentherus Zainer (?), fo. ed. of 167 leaves. (*Ger-
man :* see Herv., 1. 351–354 ; 4. 389–391 ; Brunet,
Vol. I, col. 100.)

45. (ab. 1480) **Vincentius Bellovacensis,** *Speculum
Doctrinale,* Argentorati (?), Johannes Mentellin (?),
fo. ed. (*Latin :* see Herv., 1. 395 ; 4. 449.)

46. (ab. 1480) **Vincentius Bellovacensis,** *Speculum
Historiale,* Argentorati (?), Johannes Mentellin (?),
fo. ed. (*Latin :* see Herv., 1. 395 ; 4. 449.)

47. (1481) **Accio Zuccho,** *Libellus Zucharinus,* Venetiis,
Manfredus de Monteferato, 4to ed. of 72 leaves.*
(*Latin and Italian :* see Herv., 1. 566 ; 4. 655–656 ;†
Brunet, Vol. I, col. 97.)

48. (1481) **Gualterus Anglicus,** *Esopus Moralisatus,*
Brixiae, 4to ed. (*Latin :* see Herv., 1. 545 ; 4. 604.)

---

* In his first volume Hervieux says that the edition is a folio.
† In his fourth volume Hervieux gives the date as 1491 in Venetian
reckoning, equivalent to 1492 in our reckoning, both of which see.

49. (1481) **Gualterus Anglicus,** *Esopus Moralisatus,*
Monte Regali, Dominicus de Vivaldis et Filii, fo.
ed. of 30 leaves. (*Latin:* see Herv., 1. 545; 4.
604; Brunet, Vol. I, col. 89.)

50. (1481) **Gualterus Anglicus,** *Esopus Moralisatus,*
Mutine, Thomas Septemcastrensis et Ioannes Franciscus, 4to ed. (*Latin:* see Herv., 1. 440 and 545;
4. 485 and 604; Brunet, Vol. I, col. 89.)

51. (1481) **Nicolaus Pergamenus,** *Dialogus Creatu-
rarum,* Goudae, Gerardus Leeu, fo. ed. of 103
leaves. (*Latin:* see Herv., 1. 340; 4. 377–378;
Brunet, Vol. II, cols. 674 and 676.)

52. (1481) **Nicolaus Pergamenus,** *Dialogus Creatu-
rarum,* Coloniae, Conradus de Hamborch, fo. ed.
of 62 leaves. (*Latin:* see Brunet, Vol. II, col.
674; Brunet, *Suppl.,* Vol. I, col. 388.)

53. (1481) **Nicolaus Pergamenus,** *Dialogus Creatu-
rarum,* Gouda, Gheraert Leeu, fo. ed. of 125
leaves. (*Flemish:* see Brunet, Vol. II, col. 676.)

54. (1482) **Colard Mansion,** *Dyalogue des Creatures,*
Gouwe, Gerart Lyon, fo. ed. of 101 leaves.
(*French:* see Herv., 1. 340; 4. 377; Brunet, Vol.
II, cols. 675–676; Brunet, *Suppl.,* Vol. I, col. 388.)*

55. (1482) **Gualterus Anglicus,** *Esopus Moralisatus,*
Venetiis. (*Latin and Italian:* see Herv., 1. 572.)†

56. (1482) **Hainricus Stainhöwel,** Goudae, Gerardus
Leeu, 4to ed. (*Latin:* see Herv., 1. 340; 4. 377;
Brunet, Vol. I, cols. 91 and 585.)

57. (1482) **Julien Macho,** Lyon (?), Mathis Husz et
Jehan Schabeller (?), fo. ed. of 72 leaves. (*French:*
see Herv., 1. 365–367; 4. 403–406.)‡

---

* Says 102 leaves.
† In his fourth volume Hervieux has omitted all reference to this
edition.
‡ In his fourth volume Hervieux attributes it to a date earlier than
1480 (which see), and to the printers Nicolas Philippi and Marc Reinhardi.

58. (1482) **Nicolaus Pergamenus,** *Dialogus Creatu-rarum,* Goudae, Gerardus Leeu, fo. ed. of 103 leaves. (*Latin:* see Herv., 1. 336-340; 4. 376-378; Brunet, Vol. II, cols. 674 and 676.)

59. (1482) **Nicolaus Pergamenus,** *Dialogus Creatu-rarum,* Gouda, Gheraert Leeu, fo. ed. (*Flemish:* see Herv., 1. 340; 4. 377; Brunet, Vol. II, col. 676.)

60. (ab. 1482) **Bonus Accursius,** Mediolani, Bonus Ac-cursius, 4to ed. of 38 leaves. (*Greek and Latin:* see *B. M. Æsop,* col. 5.)

61. (1483) **Accio Zuccho,** *Libellus Zucharinus,* Rome, Eucharius Silber alias Franck (?), 4to ed. of 82 leaves. (*Latin and Italian:* see Herv., 1. 566-567; 4. 653-654; Brunet, Vol. I, col. 97; *B. M. Æsop,* col. 9.)

62. (1483) **Colard Mansion,** *Dialogue des Creatures,* Lyon, Matthieu Husz et Jean Schabeller, fo. ed. (*French:* see Brunet, Vol. II, col. 676.)

63. (1483) **Franciscus de Tuppo,** Aquile, Eusanius de Stella, Joannes de Hamell et Loisius de Masson, fo. ed. of 123 leaves. (*Latin and Italian:* see Herv., 1. 572-573.)*

64. (1483) **Hainricus Stainhöwel,** Augspurg, Antho-nius Sorg, fo. ed. of 196 leaves.† (*German:* see Herv., 1. 357-358; 4. 394-395; Brunet, Vol. I, col. 101.)

65. (1483) **Nicolaus Pergamenus,** *Dialogus Creatura-rum,* Stockolm, Johannes Snell, 4to ed. (*Latin:* see Brunet, Vol. II, col. 674.)

---

* In his fourth volume Hervieux has omitted all reference to this edition.

† A copy of this edition is preserved in the library of the Johns Hop-kins University, and has been described at length in *Modern Language Notes,* Vol. XI, cols. 46-48 : George C. Keidel, *An Early German Edition of Æsop's Fables.*

66. (1483) **Vincentius Bellovacensis,** *Speculum Historiale,* Nurmberge, Antonius Koburger, fo. ed. (*Latin:* see Herv., I. 397; 4. 451; Brunet, Vol. V, col. 1255.)

67. (1484) **Julien Macho,** Lyon, Mathis Hucz et Jean Schabeller, fo. ed. (*French:* see Herv., I. 367-368; 4. 407-408; Brunet, Vol. I, col. 93.)

68. (1484) **Vincentius Bellovacensis,** *Speculum Doctrinale,* Venetiis. (*Latin:* see Herv., I. 398; 4. 452; Brunet, Vol. V, col. 1255.)

69. (1484) **Vincentius Bellovacensis,** *Speculum Historiale,* Venetiis. (*Latin:* see Herv., I. 398; 4. 452; Brunet, Vol. V, col. 1255.)

70. (1484) **William Caxton,** *Esope,* Westmynstre, William Caxton, fo. ed. of 142 leaves. (*English:* see Herv., I. 373-374; 4. 413-414; Brunet, Vol. I, col. 102; *B. M. Æsop,* col. 18.)

71. (ab. 1484) **Hainricus Stainhöwel,** Augustae (?), Erhardt Ratdolt (?), fo. ed. of 114 leaves. (*Latin:* see Herv., I. 327-333; 4. 366-370; *B. M. Æsop,* col. 13.)

72. (1485) **Francisco del Tuppo,** Neapoli, Matteo Moravo (?), fo. ed. of 168 leaves. (*Latin and Italian:* see Herv., I. 573; 4. 662-663; Brunet, Vol. I, col. 98; Brunet, *Suppl.,* Vol. I, col. 14; *B. M. Æsop,* col. 9.)

73. (1485) **Hainricus Stainhöwel,** Augspurg, Johannes Schobsser, fo. ed. (*German:* see Herv., I. 358; 4. 395-396; Brunet, Vol. I, col. 101.)

74. (1485) **Hainricus Stainhöwel,** Gouda, Gheraert Leeu, 4to ed. (*Flemish:* see Herv., I. 375-376; 4. 418.)

75. (1485) **Hainricus Stainhöwel,** Antwerpen, Gheraert Leeu, fo. ed. of 112 leaves. (*Flemish:* see Herv., I. 376; 4. 418-419; Brunet, Vol. I, col. 101.)

76. (ab. 1485) **Bonus Accursius,** Romae (?), Eucharius
    Silber alias Franck (?), 4to ed. of 44 leaves.
    (*Latin:* see *B. M. Æsop,* col. 12.)
77. (ab. 1485) **Gualterus Anglicus,** *Esopus Moralisatus,*
    4to ed. of 20 leaves. (*Latin:* see Brunet, Vol. I,
    col. 88.)
78. (ab. 1485) **Hainricus Stainhöwel,** Argentorati (?),
    Heinrich Knoblotzer (?), fo. ed. of 114 leaves.
    (*Latin:* see Herv., 1. 333-336; 4. 373-377; *B. M.
    Æsop,* col. 12.)
79. (1486) **Gualterus Anglicus,** *Esopus Moralisatus,*
    Bononiae, Ugo Rugerius, 4to ed. of 18 leaves.
    (*Latin:* see Herv., 1. 546; 4. 605; Brunet, Vol. I,
    col. 89.)
80. (1486) **Hainricus Stainhowel,** Antwerpie, Gerardus
    Leeu, fo. ed. of 104 leaves. (*Latin:* see Herv., 1.
    340-343; 4. 377-380; Brunet, Vol. I, cols. 90 and
    585; *B. M. Æsop,* col. 12.)
81. (1486) **Julien Macho,** Lyon, Mathis Husz, 4to ed.
    (*French:* see Herv., 1. 368-369; 4. 408-409; Bru-
    net, Vol. I, col. 93.)*
82. (1486) **Nicolaus Pergamenus,** *Dyalogus Creatura-
    rum,* Antwerpiae, Gerardus Leeu, fo. ed. of 74
    leaves. (*Latin:* see Brunet, Vol. II, cols. 674-
    675; Brunet, *Suppl.,* Vol. I, col. 388.)
83. (1486) **Nicolaus** Pergamenus, *Dialogus Creatura-
    rum,* Gouda, Gheraert Leeu, fo. ed. (*Flemish:* see
    Brunet, Vol. II, col. 676.)
84. (1486) **Vincentius Bellovacensis,** *Speculum Doc-
    trinale,* Nurembergk, Anthonius Koberger, fo. ed.
    (*Latin:* see Herv., 1. 398; 4. 452; Brunet, Vol.
    V, col. 1255.)
85. (1487) **Accio Zuccho,** *Libellus Zucharinus,* Brixie,
    Boninus de Boninis, 4to ed. of 100 leaves. (*Latin*

---

* Says folio edition.

and Italian: see Herv., 1. 567–568; 4. 654–655; Brunet, Vol. I, col. 97 ; *B. M. Æsop,* col. 10.)

86. (1487) **Bonus Accursius,** Rome, Eucharius Silber alias Franck, 4to ed. of 19 leaves. (*Latin:* see *B. M. Æsop,* col. 12.)

87. (1487) **Gualterus Anglicus,** *Esopus Moralisatus,* Antverpiae, 4to ed. (*Latin:* see Herv., 1. 546 ; 4. 605.)

88. (1487) **Gualterus Anglicus,** *Esopus Moralisatus,* 4to ed. (*Latin:* see Herv., 1. 546 ; 4. 605.)

89. (1487) **Hainricus Stainhöwel,** Augspurg, Johannes Schobsser, fo. ed. (*German:* see Herv., 1. 358 ; 4. 396 ; Brunet, Vol. I, col. 101.)

90. (ab. 1487) **Hainricus Stainhöwel,** Prague, 4to ed. (*Bohemian:* see Brunet, Vol. I, col. 101.)

91. (1488) **Gualterus Anglicus,** *Esopus Moralisatus,* Antverpiae (?), Gerardus Leeu, 4to ed. of 34 leaves. (*Latin:* see Herv., 1. 546–547; 4. 605 ; Brunet, Vol. I, col. 91 ; *B. M. Æsop,* col. 13.)

92. (1488) **Gualterus Anglicus,** *Esopus Moralisatus,* Lugd., Joan. de Prato, 4to ed. (*Latin:* see Herv., 1. 547; 4. 478 and 607.)*

93. (1488) **Nicolaus Pergamenus,** *Dialogus Creaturarum,* Delf, fo. ed. (*Flemish:* see Brunet, Vol. II, col. 676.)

94. (ab. 1488) **Hainricus Stainhöwel,** Parisiis, Petrus Leuet, 4to ed. (*Latin:* see Brunet, Vol. I, col. 90.)

95. (1489) **Gualterus Anglicus,** *Esopus Moralizatus,* 4to ed. of 42 leaves. (*Latin:* see Herv., 1. 547 ; 4. 608 ; *B. M. Æsop,* col. 13.)

96. (1489) **Gualterus Anglicus,** *Esopus Moralisatus,* 4to ed. of 33 leaves. (*Latin:* see Herv., 1. 547 ; 4. 608 ; *B. M. Æsop,* col. 13.)†

---

* In his first volume Hervieux gives the printer's name as Joan. de Fabro ; in his fourth volume, p. 478, by a typographical error the date is given as 1884.

† Hervieux gives the number of leaves as 32.

97. (1489) **Gualterus Anglicus,** *Esopus Moralizatus,*
Brixie, Boninus de Boninis, 4to ed. (*Latin :* see
Herv., I. 547 ; 4. 608.)

98. (1489) **Hainricus Stainhöwel,** *Ysopete Ystoriado,*
Zaragoça, Johan Hurus Alaman de Costancia, fo.
ed. of 120 leaves. (*Spanish :* see Herv., I. 379 ;
4. 421–424 ; Brunet, Vol. I, col. 99.)*

99. (1489) **Hainricus Stainhöwel,** Tolosa, fo. ed.
(*Spanish :* see Brunet, Vol. I, col. 99.)†

100. (1490) **Accio Zuccho,** *Libellus Zucharinus,* Venetia,
Manfredo da Montefera, 4to ed. of 71 leaves.
(*Latin and Italian :* see Brunet, Vol. I, col. 97.)

101. (1490) **Gualterus Anglicus,** *Esopus Moralisatus,*
Lugduni, Johannes Fabri, 4to ed. of 286 leaves.
(*Latin :* see Herv., I. 447–448 and 543–544 ; 4.
492 and 608–609.)‡

102. (1490) **Gualterus Anglicus,** *Esopus Moralizatus,*
Dauantrie (?), Jacobus de Breda (?), 4to ed. of 38
leaves. (*Latin :* see Herv., I. 547–548 ; 4. 609 ;
B. M. Æsop, col. 13.)

103. (1490) **Gualterus Anglicus,** *Esopus Moralisatus,*
Dauantrie, Jacobus de Breda, 4to ed. of 31 leaves.
(*Latin :* see Herv., I. 548 and 555 ; 4. 609 and 618.)

104. (1490) **Gualterus Anglicus,** *Esopus Moralisatus,*
Coloniae, Quentel, 4to ed. (*Latin :* see Herv.,
4. 609.)

105. (ab. 1490) **Accio Zuccho,** *Libellus Zucharinus,*
Mediolani (?), Fratres Guillermi le Signerre (?), 4to
ed. (*Latin and Italian :* see Herv., I. 568–569.)§

---

* Cf. A. Morel-Fatio, *L'Isopo Castillan,* in *Romania,* Vol. XXIII, pp.
561–575 (especially p. 563, Note 1).

† Cf. A. Morel-Fatio, *l. c.,* p. 564.

‡ In both of the references in his first volume Hervieux gives the date
as 1480, which see.

§ In his fourth volume Hervieux has omitted all reference to this
edition.

106. (ab. 1490) **Gabrielis Bracii** (?), 4to ed. (*Greek and Latin:* see Brunet, Vol. I, col. 84.)

107. (ab. 1490) **Gualterus Anglicus,** *Esopus Moralisatus,* 4to ed. of 38 leaves. (*Latin:* see Herv., 1. 448; 4. 492.)

108. (ab. 1490) **Gualterus Anglicus,** *Esopus Moralisatus,* Parisiis (?), 4to ed. of 5 leaves. (*Latin:* see Herv., 1. 448; 4. 493.)

109. (ab. 1490) **Gualterus Anglicus,** *Esopus Moralisatus,* 4to ed. of 56 leaves. (*Latin:* see Herv., 4. 493.)

110. (ab. 1490) **Gualterus Anglicus,** *Esopus Moralisatus,* 4to ed. of 20 leaves. (*Latin:* see Herv., 4. 607; Brunet, Vol. I, col. 88.)

111. (ab. 1490) **Gualterus Anglicus,** *Esopus Moralisatus,* Parisiis (?), 4to ed. of 40 leaves. (*Latin:* see *B. M. Æsop,* col. 13.)

112. (ab. 1490) **Guillaume Tardif,** *Apologues et Fables,* Paris, Antoine Verard, fo. ed. of 36 leaves. (*French:* see Brunet, Vol. V, col. 1056.)

113. (ab. 1490) **Hainricus Stainhöwel,** fo. ed. of 180 leaves. (*German:* see Brunet, Vol. I, cols. 100–101.)

114. (ab. 1490) **Julien Macho,** Lyon, Pierre Mareschal et Barnabbe Chaussard, 4to ed. of 77 leaves. (*French:* see Herv., 4. 409; *B. M. Æsop,* col. 25.)*

115. (ab. 1490) **Laurentius Valla,** *Facecie Morales,* Dauentrie, Jacobus de Breda, 4to ed. of 6 leaves. (*Latin:* see *B. M. Æsop,* col. 13.)

116. (ab. 1490) **Vincentius Bellovacensis,** *Speculum Historiale,* Westminster (?), William Caxton, ed. of 100 leaves. (*English:* see Herv., 1. 406; 4. 460.)

117. (1491) **Accio Zuccho,** *Libellus Zucharinus,* Venetiis, Manfredus de Monteferato, 4to ed. of 72 leaves.

---

* This edition is assigned by the last-mentioned work to the year 1510.

(*Latin and Italian:* see Herv., 1. 566; 4. 655–656;
Brunet, Vol. I, col. 97.)*

118. (1491) **Gualterus Anglicus,** *Esopus Moralisatus,*
Antverpiae, Gerardus Leeu. (*Latin:* see Herv.,
1. 548; 4. 610.)

119. (1491) **Gualterus Anglicus,** *Esopus Moralizatus,*
4to ed. (*Latin:* see Herv., 1. 548; 4. 610.)

120. (1491) **Gualterus Anglicus,** *Esopus Moralisatus,*
Engolisme, 4to ed. (*Latin:* see Herv., 4. 610.)

121. (1491) **Hainricus Stainh wel,** Augspurg, Hann-
sen Schönsperger, fo. ed. of 151 leaves. (*German:*
see Herv., 1. 358–359; 4. 396–397; Brunet, Vol. I,
col. 101.)

122. (1491) **Nicolaus Pergamenus,** *Dialogus Creatu-
rarum,* Antverpiae, Gerardus Leeu, 4to ed. (*Latin:*
see Brunet, Vol. II, col. 675.)

123. (ab. 1491) **Gualterus Anglicus,** *Esopus Moralisatus,*
Parisiis (?), 4to ed. of 42 leaves. (*Latin:* see
Herv., 1. 448; 4. 492; *B. M. Æsop,* col. 13.)†

124. (1492) **Accio Zuccho,** *Libellus Zucharinus,* Venetiis,
Manfredus de Monteferato, 4to ed. of 72 leaves.
(*Latin and Italian:* see Herv., 1. 566; 4. 655–656;
Brunet, Vol. I, col. 97.)‡

125. (1492) **Franciscus de Tuppo,** Venetiis, Manfredus
de Monteferato, 4to ed. (*Latin and Italian:* see
Herv., 1. 573; Brunet, Vol. I, col. 96.)§

---

* In his first volume Hervieux says that the edition is a folio. The
date here given is found in the printer's colophon and is according to
Venetian reckoning; in our own this is equivalent to 1492, which see
(as also 1481).

† Hervieux assigns no date to this edition; the last-mentioned work
assigns it to 1490, but from the other statements there made I should be
inclined to assign it rather to the following year at the very earliest.

‡ This edition was published in 1491 according to Venetian reckoning;
in his first volume Hervieux says that the edition is a folio and gives
the date as 1481, which see (as also 1491).

§ In his fourth volume Hervieux has omitted all reference to this
edition.

126. (1492) **Gualterus Anglicus,** *Esopus Moralisatus,* Anthonius Lambillon, 4to ed. (*Latin:* see Herv., 1. 448 and 548–549; 4. 610.)*

127. (1492) **Gualterus Anglicus,** *Esopus Moralisatus,* 4to ed. of 36 leaves. (*Latin:* see Herv., 1. 548; 4. 610–611.)

128. (1492) **Laurentius Valla,** *Facecie Morales,* Dauentriae (?), Jacobus de Breda (?), 4to ed. of 36 leaves. (*Latin:* see *B. M. Æsop,* col. 14.)

129. (1492) **Omnibonus Leonicenus,** Brixiae (?), Baptista de Farfengo, 4to ed. of 22 leaves. (*Latin:* see Brunet, Vol. I, cols. 89–90; *B. M. Æsop,* col. 14.)

130. (ab. 1492) **Laurentius Valla,** *Facecie Morales,* Antwerpie, Go. Bac., 4to ed. of 6 leaves. (*Latin:* see *B. M. Æsop,* col. 13.)

131. (1493) **Accio Zuccho,** *Libellus Zucharinus,* Venetiis, Manfredus de Monteferrato, 4to ed. of 72 leaves. (*Latin and Italian:* see Herv., 1. 569; 4. 656–657.)

132. (1493) **Franciscus de Tuppo,** Aquile, Eusanius de Stella, Ioannes de Hamell et Loisius de Masson, fo. ed. of 168 leaves. (*Latin and Italian:* see Herv., 1. 573; 4. 663–665.)

133. (1493) **Francisco del Tuppo,** Aquile, Eusanius de Stella, Ioannes de Hamell et Loisius de Masson, fo. ed. of 159 leaves. (*Latin and Italian:* see Herv., 1. 573; 4. 665; Brunet, Vol. I, col. 98.)

134. (1493) **Francisco del Tuppo,** Venetiis, Manfredus de Monteferato, 4to ed. (*Latin and Italian:* see Herv., 1. 573; 4. 665; Brunet, Vol. I, col. 98.)

135. (1494) **Avianus,** Daventriae (?), Jacobus de Breda (?), 4to ed. of 30 leaves. (*Latin:* see Herv., 3. 121–123; Brunet, Vol. I, col. 585.)†

---

*In his fourth volume Hervieux has omitted the second reference to this edition.

†Hervieux is unable to decide as to the printer between Jacobus de Breda and Henricus Quentell; Brunet says that this edition may pos-

136. (1494) **Gualterus Anglicus,** *Esopus Moralisatus,*
    Lugduni, 4to ed. of 212 leaves. (*Latin:* see Herv.,
    I. 549; 4. 611–612.)

137. (1494) **Gualterus Anglicus,** *Esopus Moralisatus,*
    Lugduni, Mathias Husz. (*Latin:* see Herv., I.
    448 and 550; 4. 612.)*

138. (1494) **Gualterus Anglicus,** *Esopus Moralisatus,*
    Haguenau (?), Henricus Gran (?), 4to ed. of 36
    leaves. (*Latin:* see Herv., I. 550 and 552; 4. 612–
    613 and 615; *B. M. Æsop,* col. 14.)

139. (1494) **Gualterus Anglicus,** *Esopus Moralisatus,*
    Dauentrie, Jacobus de Breda, 4to ed. of 39 leaves.
    (*Latin:* see Herv., I. 550–551; 4. 613; Brunet,
    Suppl., Vol. I, col. 14.)

140. (1494) **Vincentius Bellovacensis,** *Speculum Doc-
    trinale,* Venetiis, Hermannus Liechtenstein, fo. ed.
    of 255 leaves. (*Latin:* see Herv., I. 399; 4. 453;
    Brunet, Vol. V, col. 1255.)

141. (1494) **Vincentius Bellovacensis,** *Speculum His-
    toriale,* Venetiis, Hermannus Liechtenstein, fo. ed.
    (*Latin:* see Herv., I. 400; 4. 453–454; Brunet,
    Vol. V, col. 1255.)

142. (1495) **Gualterus Anglicus,** *Esopus Moralisatus,*
    Dauentrie, Jacobus de Breda, 4to ed. (*Latin:* see
    Herv., I. 551; 4. 613.)

143. (1495) **Jehan de Vignay,** *Miroir Historial,* Paris,
    Anthoine Verard, fo. ed. of 332 leaves. (*French:*
    see Herv., I. 401–404; 4. 455–456; Brunet, Vol.
    V, col. 1256.)

144. (1495) **Laurentius Abstemius,** Venetiis, Joannes
    de Cereto, 4to ed. of 29 leaves. (*Latin:* see Brunet,
    Vol. I, col. 16.)

---

sibly contain only 26 leaves and have been printed by Henr. Quentell
at Cologne.

 * In his fourth volume Hervieux has omitted the first reference to this
edition.

145. (ab. 1495) **Gualterus Anglicus,** *Esopus Moralisatus,*
Dauantriæ, Richardus Pafroed, 4to ed. of 37 leaves.
(*Latin:* see Herv., 1. 552; 4. 615.)

146. (ab. 1495) **Gualterus Anglicus,** *Esopus Moralisatus,*
4to ed. of 31 leaves. (*Latin:* see *B. M. Æsop,*
col. 14.)

147. (ab. 1495) **Gualterus Anglicus,** *Esopus Moralisatus,*
Parisiis (?), Andreas Bocard (?), 4to ed. of 35 leaves.
(*Latin:* see *B. M. Æsop,* col. 14.)

148. (ab. 1495) **Julien Macho,** fo. ed. of 88 leaves.
(*French:* see Herv., 1. 369–370; 4. 406 ; Brunet,
Vol. I, col. 93 ; *B. M. Æsop,* col. 25.)*

149. (ab. 1495) **Laurentius Valla,** *Facecie Morales,*
Dauentriæ, Jacobus de Breda, 4to ed. of 6 leaves.
(*Latin:* see *B. M. Æsop,* col. 14.)

150. (1496) **Gualterus Anglicus,** *Esopus Moralisatus,*
Dauentrie, Jacobus de Breda, 4to ed. of 38 leaves.
(*Latin:* see Herv., 1. 551; 4. 613–614; *B. M.*
Æsop, col. 14.)

151. (1496) **Gualterus Anglicus,** *Esopus Moralisatus,*
Mediolani, Philippus de Mantegatiis, 4to ed. of 18
leaves. (*Latin:* see Herv., 1. 551–552; 4. 614.)

152. (1496) **Gualterus Anglicus,** *Esopus Moralisatus,*
Lugduni, Petrus Marescalli et Barnabas Chaus-
sardi, 4to ed. (*Latin:* see Herv., 1. 448 and 552;
4. 614.)†

153. (1496) **Gualterus Anglicus,** *Esopus Moralisatus,*
Dauentrie, Richardus Paffroed, 4to ed. (*Latin:*
see Herv., 1. 552; 4. 615.)

154. (1496) **Gualterus Anglicus,** *Favole di Esopo Vol-*

---

* In his first volume Hervieux gives the number of leaves as 72, as
does Brunet; in his fourth volume Hervieux identifies this as the *editio
princeps* printed before 1480.

† In his fourth volume Hervieux has omitted the first reference to
this edition.

garizzate, Firenze, Francesco Bonaccorsi. (*Italian:* see Herv., 4. 645.)*

155. (1496) **Hainricus Stainh wel**, Augspurg, Hann-sen Schönsperger (?), fo. ed. (*German:* see Herv., 1. 359; 4. 397; Brunet, Vol. I, col. 101.)

156. (1496) **Hainricus Stainhöwel**, *Ysopo Historiado*, Burgos, Fadrique Aleman, fo. ed. of 102 leaves. (*Spanish:* see Herv., 1. 379; 4. 424; Brunet, Vol. I, cols. 99-100.)†

157. (1497) **Accio Zuccho**, *Libellus Zucharinus*, Venetia, Manfredo da Montefera, 4to ed. of 72 leaves. (*Latin and Italian:* see Herv., 1. 569; 4. 657-658; Brunet, Vol. I, cols. 97-98 ;‡ Brunet, *Suppl.*, Vol. I, col. 14; *B. M. Æsop*, col. 10.)

158. (1497) **Accio Zuccho**, *Libellus Zucharinus*, Medio-lani, Uldericus Scinzenzeler, 4to. ed. of 40 leaves. (*Latin and Italian:* see Herv., 1. 569; 4. 658.)

159. (1497) **Bonus Accursius**, Regii, Dionysius Ber-tochus, 4to ed. of 38 leaves. (*Greek and Latin:* see Brunet, Vol. I, col. 84; *B. M. Æsop*, col. 5.)

160. (1497) **Gualterus Anglicus**, *Esopus Moralisatus*, Coloniæ (?), Henricus Quentell (?), 4to ed. of 40 leaves. (*Latin:* see Herv., 1. 552-553; 4. 615; *B. M. Æsop*, col. 14.)§

161. (1497) **Gualterus Anglicus**, *Esopus Moralisatus*, Brixiæ (?), Bernardinus de Misuitis, 4to ed. of 36 leaves. (*Latin and Italian:* see Herv., 1. 553; 4. 615-616; Brunet, Vol. I, col. 91; *B. M. Æsop*, col. 14.)

162. (1497) **Gualterus Anglicus**, *Esopus Moralisatus*, 4to ed. (*Latin:* see Herv., 1. 553; 4. 616.)

---

* This edition includes the translations of both Accio Zuccho and the Anonimo Senese.

† Cf. A. Morel-Fatio, *L'Isopo Castillan*, in *Romania*, Vol. XXIII, pp. 561-575.

‡ Says 71 leaves.

§ Hervieux says 39 leaves.

163. (ab. 1497) **Sebastianus Brandt**, Moguntiaci (?), P. Schoeffer (?), fo. ed. of 75 leaves. (*Latin :* see Brunet, Vol. I, col. 91.)

164. (1498) **Accio Zuccho**, *Libellus Zucharinus*, Mediolani, Guillermus le Signerre, 4to ed. of 70 leaves. (*Latin and Italian :* see Herv., 1. 569; 4. 658-659; *B. M. Æsop*, col. 10.)

165. (1498) **Gabrielis Bracii**, Venetiis, 4to ed. of 48 leaves. (*Greek:* see Brunet, Vol. I, col. 84; *B. M. Æsop*, col. 1.)

166. (1498) **Gualterus Anglicus**, *Esopus Moralisatus*, Dauentriæ, Jacobus de Breda. (*Latin :* see Herv., 1. 553; 4. 616.)

167. (1498) **Gualterus Anglicus**, *Esopus Moralisatus*, Lugduni, Nicolaus Lupi (?), 4to ed. of 186 leaves. (*Latin :* see Herv., 1. 553; 4. 616-617.)

168. (1498) **Gualterus Anglicus**, *Esopus Moralisatus*, Lugduni (?), Nicolaus Lupi (?), 4to ed. (*Latin :* see Herv., 1. 554; 4. 617.)

169. (1498) **Hainricus Stainhöwel**, Augspurg, Hannssen Schönsperger, fo. ed. of 105 leaves. (*German :* see Herv., 1. 359-360; 4. 397; Brunet, Vol. I, col. 101.)

170. (1498) **Hainricus Stainhöwel**, Delf, Henrick Eckert van Homberch, fo. ed. of 100 leaves. (*Flemish :* see Herv., 1. 376-378; 4. 419-421; Brunet, Vol. I, col. 101; *B. M. Æsop*, col. 24.)

171. (1499) **Gualterus Anglicus**, *Esopus Moralisatus*, Parisiis, Petrus Leuet, 4to ed. of 36 leaves. (*Latin :* see Herv., 1. 448 and 554; 4. 493 and 617.)

172. (1499) **Julien Macho**, Lyon, Pierre Mareschal et Barnabbe Chaussard, 4to ed. of 77 leaves. (*French :* see Herv., 1. 369; 4. 409; Brunet, Vol. I, col. 93.)

173. (1499) **Laurentius Abstemius**, Venetiis, Joannes de Cereto, 4to ed. of 28 leaves. (*Latin :* see Brunet, Vol. I, cols. 15-16.)

174. (1500) **Bonus Accursius,** Florentiæ. (*Greek and Latin :* see Cat. Carlsruhe Libr.)*

175. (1500) **Gualterus Anglicus,** *Esopus Moralisatus,* Dauentrie, Jacobus de Breda, 4to ed. of 40 leaves. (*Latin :* see Herv., 1. 554–555 ; 4. 618.)

176. (1500) **Gualterus Anglicus,** *Esopus Moralisatus,* 4to ed. of 92 leaves. (*Latin :* see Herv., 4. 618–619.)

177. (1500) **Nicolaus Pergamenus,** *Dialogus Creaturarum,* Genevæ (?), Jehan Bellot (?), fo. ed. (*Latin :* see Brunet, Vol. II, col. 675.)

178. (ab. 1500) **William Caxton,** *Esope,* London (?), R. Pynson, fo. ed. of 94 leaves at least. (*English :* see Herv., 1. 374 ; 4. 414 ; *B. M. Æsop,* col. 19.)

EXTANT COPIES.†

1. **Ulrich Boner:**
   a. Wolfenbüttel, *Herzogliche Bibl.,* (?).‡
2. **Ulrich Boner:**
   a. Berlin, *Königliche Bibl.,* (?).§
3. **Laurentius Valla:**
   a. Amsterdam, *Enschedé Sale,* 400 *fl.*‖
   b. Haarlem, *Bibl. Comunale,* (?).‖
   c. London, *British Museum,* G. 7722.
4. **Vincentius Bellovacensis:**
   a. London, *Kloss Sale,* 1835, (?).

---

* *Katalog der Grossherzoglichen Badischen Hof- und Landesbibliothek in Carlsruhe.* Zweite Abtheilung, Vierter Band. Carlsruhe : Druck und Verlag von Ch. Th. Groos, 1877. 8vo, pp. 308-593. See p. 530.

† Owing to the great difficulty of identifying editions and descriptions of Incunabula, much of the information given in this, as well as in the preceding list, is to be regarded as merely tentative and hence peculiarly liable to correction.

‡ Seen by Brunet.

§ In March of 1835, Brunet saw this copy, for which M. Pieri Benard, a bookseller of Paris, asked 3000 *fr.*

‖ 3*a* and 3*b* are identical.

5. **Vincentius Bellovacensis:**
   a. London, *Kloss Sale*, 1835, (?).
6. **Omnibonus Leonicenus:**
   a. London, *British Museum*, C. 1. a. 2.
7. **Bonus Accursius:**
   a. London, *Bernard Quaritch Cat.*, 1886, £100.*
   b. Paris, *Yéméniz Sale*, 1868, 1100 *fr.*
8. **Gualterus Anglicus:**
   a. London, *Sykes Sale*, 1824, £14 3s. 6d.
   b. London, *Thorold Sale*, 1884.†
9. **Vincentius Bellovacensis:**
   a. Boston, *Boston Public Libr.*, B. 150. 3.‡
   b. London, *Kloss Sale*, 1835, (?).
   c. Paris, *Bibl. Nationale*, (?).§
   d. Paris, *MacCarthy Sale*, 1779, 685 *fr.*‖

---

*Cf.: 1. *Monuments of the Early Printers in All Countries*; preceded by some examples of the Art of Xylography. Part I: Germany and the Low Countries. Offered for cash at the affixed net prices by Bernard Quaritch, 15 Piccadilly, W. London, December, 1886. 8vo, pp. 3527–3622. See p. 3555, No. 36052.

2. *Book-Binding: A Catalogue of Fifteen Hundred Books Remarkable for the Beauty or the Age of Their Bindings, or as Bearing Indications of Former Ownership by Great Book-Collectors and Famous Historical Personages;* now on sale at 15 Piccadilly. Bernard Quaritch, London, November, 1888. 8vo, 200 pp. See p. 103, No. 754.

†Cf. *Catalogue of an Important Portion of the Extensive and Valuable Library of the Late Sir John Hayford Thorold, Bart., Removed from Syston Park, Lincolnshire,* which will be sold by auction by Messrs. Sotheby, Wilkinson (and) Hodge at their house, No. 13 Wellington Street, Strand, W. C. (London), 1884. 8vo, vii and 193 pp. See p. 5, No. 36.

‡Cf. *Index to the Catalogue of Books in the Bates Hall of the Public Library of the City of Boston.* First Supplement. Boston: J. E. Farwell (and) Co., Printers to the City, No. 37 Congress Street, 1866. 8vo, v, 718 and 21 pp. See p. 673, col. 2.

§Seen by Deschamps, or G. Brunet.

‖Brunet states that this set consists of ten volumes and was later offered for sale at 700 *fr.*

10. **Vincentius Bellovacensis:**
    - *a.* London, *Kloss Sale*, 1835, (?).
    - *b.* Paris, *Andry Sale*, 1830, 299 *fr.**
    - *c.* Paris, *Hervieux' Libr.*†
    - *d.* Paris, *MacCarthy Sale*, 1779, 685 *fr.*‡
    - *e.* Paris, *Morante Sale*, 205 *fr.*†
    - *f.* Paris, *Soubise Sale*, 1788, 100 *fr.**

11. **Bonus Accursius:**
    - *a.* London, *British Museum*, C. 1. a. 1. (1.).
    - *b.* London, *British Museum*, C. 19. c. (1.).
    - *c.* London, *British Museum*, G. 7726. (2.).
    - *d.* Paris, *Brienne-Laire Sale*, 1791, 30 *fr.*

12. **Vincentius Bellovacensis:**
    - *a.* Boston, *Boston Public Libr.*, B. 150. 4.§
    - *b.* Boston, *Boston Public Libr.*, B. 150. 6.§
    - *c.* Paris, *Golowkin Sale*, (?).‖

13. **Vincentius Bellovacensis:**
    - *a.* (No copy known to me.)

14. **Gualterus Anglicus:**
    - *a.* Paris, *Brienne-Laire Sale*, 1791, 27 *fr.*

15. **Gualterus Anglicus:**
    - *a.* Stuttgart, *Kgl. Öffentliche Bibl.*, (?).¶

16. **Avianus:**
    - *a.* Paris, *Elcy Sale*, (?).

17. **Hainricus Stainhöwel:**
    - *a.* Althorp, *Earl Spencer's Libr.*, (?).**
    - *b.* Firenze, *R. Bibl. Mediceo-Laurenziana*, E. 2. 326.¶

---

* 10*b* and 10*f* are identical. Brunet states that this edition of the *Speculum Historiale* consists of four volumes.

† 10*c* and 10*e* are identical.

‡ Brunet states that this set consists of ten volumes and was later offered for sale at 700 *fr.*

§ Cf. reference given for 9*a*. See p. 674, col. 1.

‖ Brunet states that this edition of the *Speculum Historiale* consists of three volumes.

¶ Seen by Hervieux.

** 17*a* and 17*d* are identical; Earl Spencer's Library was removed to Manchester in 1893.

c. London, *Bernard Quaritch Cat.*, 1874, £15. Imperfect.*

d. Manchester, *Mrs. Rylands' Libr.*, (?).†

e. München, *Kgl. Hof- u. Staatsbibl.*, A. Gr. B. 12.‡

f. Oxford, *Bodleian Libr.*, Douce G. P. 252. Imperfect.‡

g. Wien, *K. u. K. Hofbibl.*, 3. D. 8.‡

h. Wolfenbüttel, *Herzogliche Bibl.*, 10. 2. Ethic.§

18. **Gualterus Anglicus:**
    a. (No copy known to me.)

19. **Bonus Accursius:**
    a. London, *British Museum*, G. 7727.
    b. London, *Heber Sale*, 1834–1836, £1 1s.
    c. London, *Hibbert Sale*, 1829, £12 15s.
    d. London, *Libri Sale*, 1859, £2 12s.‖
    e. London, *Pinelli Sale*, 1789, 12s. 6d.

20. **Gualterus Anglicus:**
    a. Paris, *Bibl. Nationale*, (?).

21. **Bonus Accursius:**
    a. London, *British Museum*, G. 7728.
    b. Paris, *Boutourlin Sale*, 1839–1841, (?).¶
    c. Rome, *Unspecified Sale*, 1478, 3 fr.¶

---

* Cf. *A General Catalogue of Books Offered to the Public at the Affixed Prices* by Bernard Quaritch. London : 15 Piccadilly, 1874. 8vo, x and 1889 pp. See pp. 355–356, No. 3732.

† 17a and 17d are identical ; Earl Spencer's Library was removed to Manchester in 1893.

‡ Seen by Hervieux.

§ Seen by Schwabe.

‖ This copy was bought by Mr. Leslie ; cf. a manuscript note on the margin of p. 50, No. 32, of a copy of the following catalogue now in the Library of the Johns Hopkins University (No. 42434) : *Catalogue of the Choicer Portions of the Magnificent Library Formed by M. Guglielmo Libri*, so eminent as a collector, who is leaving London in consequence of ill-health and solely for that reason disposing of his literary treasures : which will be sold by auction by Messrs. S. Leigh Sotheby (and) John Wilkinson at their house, 3 Wellington Street, Strand (London), 1859. 8vo, xx and 380 pp.

¶ 21b and 21c are identical.

22. **Gualterus Anglicus :**
     a. (No copy known to me.)
23. **Accio Zuccho :**
     a. Paris, *Boutourlin Sale*, 1839–1841, 40 *fr.* 50 *c.**
     b. Paris, *Molini Sale*, 1813, 220 *fr.**
24. **Laurentius Valla :**
     a. London, *British Museum*, 1079. m. 8.
25. **Accio Zuccho :**
     a. London, *Bernard Quaritch Cat.*, 1894, £50.†
     b. London, *British Museum*, 12305. g. 6.   Imper-
        fect.
     c. London, *British Museum*, C. 1. a. 5.‡
     d. London, *British Museum*, G. 7729.‡
     e. Paris, *Boutourlin Sale*, 1839–1841, 40 *fr.* 50 *c.**
     f. Paris, *Molini Sale*, 1813, 220 *fr.**
26. **Bonus Accursius :**
     a. (No copy known to me.)
27. **Gualterus Anglicus :**
     a. (No copy known to me.)
28. **Gualterus Anglicus :**
     a. (No copy known to me.)
29. **Jehan de Vignay :**
     a. Rio de Janeiro, *Bibl. Nacional*, 63.   Imperfect.§

---

* The identity of these copies is doubtful.

† Cf. : 1. *A Catalogue of Greek (and) Latin Classics, Modern Latinists, Works on Classical Philology, History and Archæology ;* offered by Bernard Quaritch, 15 Piccadilly, London, September, 1893. 8vo, viii and 136 pp. See p. 2, No. 14.

2. *A Catalogue of Italian Literature, Art, Archæology and History ;* offered by Bernard Quaritch, 15 Piccadilly, London, April 15th, 1894. 8vo, 120 pp. See p. 6, No. 126, and pp. 84–85, No. 1149.

This copy formerly belonged to Mr. Fountaine Walker.

‡ Seen by Hervieux.

§ Cf. *Catalogo da Exposição Permanente dos Cimelios da Bibliotheca Nacional,* publicado sob a direcção do Bibliothecario João de Saldanha da Gama. Rio de Janeiro : typ. de G. Leuzinger (e) Filhos, Rua do Ouvidor 31, 1885. 8vo, 1071 pp. and 5 plates. See p. 163.

30. **Julien Macho :**
    a. London, *British Museum*, G. 7806.*
31. **Bonus Accursius :**
    a. London, *British Museum*, G. 7731.
    b. Paris, *Salle Silvestre*, 1809, 25 *fr.*
32. **Franciscus Philelphus :**
    a. London, *Heber Sale*, 1834–1836, £3. Imperfect.
    b. Copy seen by Robert.†
33. **Gualterus Anglicus :**
    a. Grenoble, *Bibl. Municipale*, 173.
    b. Würzburg, *Universitätsbibl.*, L. R. 9. 44.‡
34. **Julien Macho :**
    a. Tours, *Bibl. Municipale*, 3266.
35. **Nicolaus Pergamenus :**
    a. Amsterdam, *Meermann Sale*, 50 *fl.*
    b. Darmstadt, *Grossherzogl. Hofbibl.*, (?).§
    c. London, *Beckford Sale*, 1882.‖
    d. London, *Bernard Quaritch Cat.*, 1886, £20.¶
       Imperfect.
    e. London, *Bernard Quaritch Cat.*, 1886, £40.**

---

* Seen by Hervieux; his account of this book and that given by the printed catalogue, col. 25, are at variance as to its identity.
† Cf. description of his work given on p. 2 of this *Manual.* See Vol. I, p. ccxlvii.
‡ Seen by Hervieux.
§ Cf. *Neue Beiträge zur Näheren Kenntniss der Grossherzoglichen Hofbibliothek in Darmstadt*, von Dr. Ph. A. F. Walther. Darmstadt : Verlag von Johann Philipp Diehl, 1871. 8vo, xv and 168 pp. See p. 40, No. 17.
‖ Cf. *The Hamilton Palace Libraries : Catalogue of the First Portion of the Beckford Library, Removed from Hamilton Palace*, which will be sold by auction by Messrs. Sotheby, Wilkinson (and) Hodge at their house, No. 13 Wellington Street, Strand, W. C. (London), 1882. 8vo, v and 237 pp. See p. 201, No. 2741.
¶ Cf. reference given for 7a (1.). See p. 3603, No. 36274.
** Cf. reference given for 7a (1.). See p. 3603, No. 36275; the signatures of Thomas Ireland, Nicholas Stokesley, Bartholomew Kirkbye and Robert Thacker, all written in this volume between 1490 and 1570, attest its early arrival in England. There are a few English glosses in the writing of the earliest owner, Thomas Ireland.

f. London, *Bernard Quaritch Cat.*, 1886, £63.*

g. London, *British Museum*, C. 38. h. 3.†

h. London, *British Museum*, G. 8989.‡

i. London, *Heber Sale*, 1834–1836, £3 7s.

j. London, *Heber Sale* (*bis*), 1834–1836, £3 14s.

k. London, *Stanley Sale*, (?), £42.§

l. London, *Sykes Sale*, 1824, £8 18s. 6d.

m. London, *Thorold Sale*, 1884, (?).§

n. Paris, *Gaignat Sale*, 1769, 96 *fr.*

o. Paris, *MacCarthy Sale*, 1779, 88 *fr.*

p. Copy seen by Robert. ‖

36. **Accio Zuccho :**

    a. Firenze, *R. Bibl. Nazionale Centrale*, Magl. 15. F. b. ¶

    b. London, *Hibbert Sale*, 1829, £6 16s. 6d.

    c. London, *Cassano Serra Sale*, (?).**

---

*Cf. reference given for 7a(1.). See p. 3603, No. 36276; this copy is bound up with the *Gesta Romanorum* of the same printer. It bears the inscription : "Pertinet in Steyn prope Goudam," first written early in the sixteenth century, and repeated elsewhere at a later date.

†Cf. *British Museum : Catalogue of Printed Books.* D'ff-Diez y Foncalda. London : printed by William Clowes and Sons, limited, Stamford Street and Charing Cross. 1887. 4to, 306 cols. See col. 22.

‡Cf. 1. Reference given for 35g. See col. 22.

2. *British Museum : A Guide to the Printed Books Exhibited to the Public,* by W. B. Rye. Printed by Order of the Trustees. London : Woodfall and Kinder, Milford Lane, Strand, W. C., 1870. 12mo, 32 pp. See p. 10.

§ 35k and 35m are identical. Cf. reference given for 8b. See p. 65, No. 672.

‖Cf. description of his work given on p. 2 of this *Manual.* See Vol. I, p. ccxlvi.

¶ Seen by Ghivizzani ; cf. *Il Volgarizzamento delle Favole di Galfredo Dette di Esopo* ; testo di lingua edito per cura di Gaetano Ghivizzani. Con un discorso intorno la origine della favola, la sua ragione storica e i fonti dei volgarizzamenti italici. Bologna : presso Gaetano Romagnoli, 1866. 12mo, ccxvii and 289 pp. See pp. cxci-cxciii. (*Scelta di Curiosità Letterarie Inedite o Rare dal Secolo xiii al xvii* ; in appendice alla *Collezione di Opere Inedite o Rare.* Dispense lxxv e lxxvi.)

**Cf. *Allgemeines Bibliographisches Lexikon,* von Friedrich Adolf Ebert. Erster Band. Leipzig : F. A. Brockhaus, 1821. 4to, xxii pp. and 1076 cols. See col. 22.

37. **Bonus Accursius:**
   a. Althorp, *Earl Spencer's Libr.*, (?).*
   b. London, *British Museum*, C. 1. a. 1. (2.).
   c. London, *British Museum*, C. 19. c. (2.).†
   d. London, *British Museum*, G. 7726. (1.).
   e. London, *Duke of Devonshire's Libr.*, (?).‡
   f. London, *Heber Sale*, 1834–1836, £6.
   g. London, *Hibbert Sale*, 1829, £9 5s.
   h. London, *Pinelli Sale*, 1789, £14.
   i. London, *Thorold Sale*, 1884.§
   j. Manchester, *Mrs. Rylands' Libr.*, (?).*
   k. Oxford, *Bodleian Libr.*, (?).‖
   l. Oxford, *Bodleian Libr.*, (?).¶
   m. Paris, *Boutourlin Sale*, 1839–1841, 185 *fr.*
   n. Paris, *La Vallière Sale*, 1767, 121 *fr.*
   o. Paris, *Libri Sale*, 1847–1858, 250 *fr.*

---

* Cf. *Caxton Celebration, 1877: Catalogue of the Loan Collection of Antiquities, Curiosities and Appliances Connected with the Art of Printing, South Kensington,* edited by George Bullen. London: printed at the Elzevir Press; published by N. Trübner and Co., Ludgate Hill. 8vo, xix and 472 pp. See p. 60, No. 432.

37*a* and 37*j* are identical. Earl Spencer's library was removed to Manchester in 1893.

† Either this copy or the preceding is probably referred to by:

1. *An Introduction to the Knowledge of Rare and Valuable Editions of the Greek and Latin Classics,* by the Rev. Thomas Frognall Dibdin. Fourth edition, greatly enlarged and corrected. Vol. I. London: 1827. 8vo, xiii and 562 pp. See pp. 245–246.

2. Cf. reference given for 35*h* (2.). See p. 12, No. 8.

The copy in question formerly belonged to the Rev. C. M. Cracherode, by whom it was bequeathed to the *British Museum.*

‡ Cf. reference given for 37*c* (1.). See pp. 245–246.

§ Cf. reference given for 8*b.* See p. 5, No. 37.

‖ Cf. 1. Reference given for 37*c* (1.). See pp. 245–246.

2. *Catalogus Librorum Impressorum Bibliothecæ Bodleianæ in Academia Oxoniensi.* Volumen Primum. Oxonii: e Typographeo Academico, 1843. fo, x and 834 pp. See p. 23, col. 1.

¶ Cf. the catalogue just cited, same reference. The two editions there mentioned are perhaps not identical.

p. Paris, *MacCarthy Sale,* 1779, 400 *fr.*
q. Washington, *Libr. of Congress,* (?).*

38. **Hainricus Stainhöwel:**
    a. London, *Heber Sale,* 1834–1836, £4 1*s.*
    b. Paris, *Brienne-Laire Sale,* 1791, 30 *fr.*
    c. Wien, *Bibl. Albertina,* (?).†
    d. Copy seen by Robert (possibly of this edition).‡

39. **Hainricus Stainhöwel:**
    a. Firenze, *R. Bibl. Mediceo-Laurenziana,* F. 2. 879.†
    b. Linz, *K. u. K. Studienbibl.,* D. iv. 9.
    c. London, *British Museum,* G. 7805.†
    d. München, *Kgl. Hof- u. Staatsbibl.,* A. Gr. B. 15.†
    e. Stuttgart, *Kgl. Öffentliche Bibl.,* (?).†
    f. Wien, *K. u. K. Hofbibl.,* V. F. 36.

40. **Hainricus Stainhöwel:**
    a. Paris, *Bibl. Nationale,* (?).
    b. Copy seen by Robert (possibly of this edition).‡

41. **Hainricus Stainhöwel:**
    a. Paris, *Bibl. Nationale,* (?).

42. **Hainricus Stainhöwel:**
    a. (No copy known to me.)

43. **Hainricus Stainhöwel:**
    a. (No copy known to me.)

---

* Cf. *Alphabetical Catalogue of the Library of Congress.* Vol. I. Washington : Government Printing Office, 1878. 4to, ii and 912 pp. See p. 85, col. 1.

On April 7, 1896, an unsuccessful attempt was made by me to verify this entry; the most that I was able to do was to make a copy of the corresponding entry in their card catalogue, where the book is described as an imperfect copy, etc., etc., preserved in the Librarian's private office. This gentleman, Mr. A. R. Spofford, kindly made a personal search for me, but was obliged to report it as "unfindable." The copy in question was acquired by the *Library of Congress* in 1875.

† Seen by Hervieux.

‡ Cf. description of his work given on p. 2 of this *Manual.* See Vol. I, p. ccxlviii.

44. **Heinricus Stainhöwel:**
    a. Paris, *Unspecified Sale*, 1856, 180 *fr.*
    b. Wien, *K. u. K. Hofbibl.*, X. E. 28.*

45. **Vincentius Bellovacensis:**
    a. Toulouse, *Bibl. du Collège*, (?).

46. **Vincentius Bellovacensis:**
    a. Toulouse, *Bibl. du Collège*, (?).

47. **Accio Zuccho:**
    a. Venezia, *Bibl. Nazionale Marciana*, CXIII. 7. 41304.*
    b. Wien, *K. u. K. Hofbibl.*, IV. H. 36.*

48. **Gualterus Anglicus:**
    a. (No copy known to me.)

49. **Gualterus Anglicus:**
    a. Paris, *Molini Sale*, 1813, 168*l.* Imperfect.

50. **Gualterus Anglicus:**
    a. Venezia, *Apostolo Zeno's Libr.*, (?).†

51. **Nicolaus Pergamenus:**
    a. London, *British Museum*, 637. k. 15.‡
    b. Paris, *Bibl. Nationale*, Y. 6592.
    c. Paris, *La Vallière Sale*, 1767, 87 *fr.*
    d. Paris, *Salle Silvestre*, 1830, 134 *fr.*

52. **Nicolaus Pergamenus:**
    a. London, *British Museum*, 637. k. 28.‡
    b. London, *British Museum*, 694. l. 17. (2.).‡
    c. London, *Heber Sale*, 1834–1836, £1 16s.
    d. London, *Thorold Sale*, 1884.§
    e. Paris, *Brienne-Laire Sale*, 1791, 14 *fr.*
    f. Paris, *Yéméniz Sale*, 1868, 400 *fr.*

---

* Seen by Hervieux.
† Seen by Morelli.
‡ Cf. reference given for 35*g.* See col. 22.
§ Cf. reference given for 8*b.* See p. 65, No. 673.

53. **Nicolaus Pergamenus :**
    a. Haag, *Martinus Nijhoff Cat.*, 1893, 50 *fl.**
    b. London, *Bernard Quaritch Cat.*, 1886, £7 10s.†
    Imperfect.
54. **Colard Mansion :**
    a. Köln, *Stadtbibl.*, (?).
    b. Paris, *Bibl. Nationale*, (?).
    c. Paris, *Yéméniz Sale*, 1868, 6000 *fr.*‡
55. **Gualterus Anglicus :**
    a. (No copy known to me.)
56. **Hainricus Stainhöwel :**
    a. (No copy known to me.)
57. **Julien Macho :**
    a. London, *British Museum*, G. 7806.§
58. **Nicolaus Pergamenus :**
    a. London, *British Museum*, C. 19. d. 5.§
    b. London, *British Museum*, C. 19. d. 26.‖
    c. Paris, *Bibl. Nationale*, (?).
    d. Windsor Castle, *Royal Libr.*, (?).¶
59. **Nicolaus Pergamenus :**
    a. Darmstadt, *Grossherzogl. Hofbibl.*, (?).**
    b. Paris, *Bibl. Nationale*, (?).
60. **Bonus Accursius :**
    a. London, *British Museum*, C. 1. a. 1. (2.).
    b. London, *British Museum*, C. 19. c. (2.).
    c. London, *British Museum*, G. 7726. (1.).

---

* Cf. *Curiosités de l'Art Typographique* (1466–1890); *Catalogue de Livres Rares et Curieux en Vente aux Prix Marqués chez Martinus Nijhoff, à la Haye.* La Haye : Martinus Nijhoff, 1893. 8vo, 81 pp. See p. 5, No. 34.

† Cf. reference given for 7*a*. See p. 3603, No. 36277.

‡ M. Yéméniz bought this copy at Ghent in 1849 for 2000 *fr.*, and then had a 1000 *fr.* binding put on it by Trautz.

§ Seen by Hervieux.

‖ Cf. reference given for 35*g*. See col. 22.

¶ Cf. reference given for 37*a*. See p. 70, No. 513.

** Cf. reference given for 35*b*. See p. 40, No. 18.

61. **Accio Zuccho :**
  a. London, *British Museum*, G. 7732.
  b. Paris, *Bibl. Nationale*, 6534 Y.*

62. **Colard Mansion :**
  a. Paris, *Du Fay Sale*, 1725, (?).†

63. **Franciscus de Tuppo :**
  a. London, *British Museum*, G. 7807.‡
  b. München, *Kgl. Hof- u. Staatsbibl.*, Inc. c. a. 2800.§

64. **Hainricus Stainhöwel :**
  a. Baltimore, *Johns Hopkins University Libr.*, 38047.‖
    Imperfect.
  b. Linz, *K. u. K. Studienbibl.*, D. iv. 9.§
  c. Stuttgart, *Kgl. Hofbibl.*, (?).§

65. **Nicolaus Pergamenus :**
  a. (No copy known to me.)

66. **Vincentius Bellovacensis :**
  a. London, *Heber Sale*, 1834–1836, £1 13s.¶
  b. Paris, *Bearzi Sale*, 1855, 190 *fr.*¶
  c. St. Gallen, *Vadianische Bibl.*, 785.**

---

* Seen by Hervieux ; this is probably the same copy as that seen by Robert, cf. description of his work given on p. 2 of this *Manual*; see Vol. I, p. ccxli.

† Cf. *Biblomania in the Present Day in France and England*; from the French of Philomneste Junior. New York, 1880. 8vo. 141 pp. See p. 14.

‡ Seen by Hervieux ; the printed catalogue, col. 9, otherwise identifies this copy.

§ Seen by Hervieux.

‖ Seen by G. C. Keidel, Dec. 11, 1895; this copy was purchased by the late John W. McCoy in 1878 at the *Strong Sale* in New York for $17.50, and was at his death in 1889 bequeathed by him to the Johns Hopkins University. Cf. *Catalogue of the Books, Manuscripts, etc., of the late George T. Strong, Esq.*, which will be sold at auction by Messrs. Bangs (and) Co., 656 Broadway, New York, 1878. 8vo, iv and 167 pp. See p. 2, No. 14, with the price of purchase given in the margin in the late owner's copy.

¶ 66*a* and 66*b* are identical. Brunet states that this set, including No. 84 of the present list, consists of four volumes.

** Cf. *Verzeichniss der Manuscripte und Incunabeln der Vadianischen Bibliothek in St. Gallen.* St. Gallen : Druck der Zollikofer'schen Offizin, 1864. 8vo, xiii and 353 pp. See p. 345.

67. **Julien Macho:**
    a. Paris, *Bibl. Nationale*, (?).   Imperfect.*
68. **Vincentius Bellovacensis:**
    a. (No copy known to me.)
69. **Vincentius Bellovacensis:**
    a. (No copy known to me.)
70. **William Caxton:**
    a. London, *British Museum*, C. 11. c. 17.†
    b. Oxford, *Bodleian Libr.*, Auct. Q. Q. supra 1. 21.‡
    c. Windsor Castle, *Royal Libr.*, (?).§
71. **Hainricus Stainhöwel:**
    a. Basel, *Museum*, B. C. iii. 7.†
    b. London, *British Museum*, 167. f. 12.†
    c. London, *British Museum*, G. 7831.†
    d. Maëstricht, *Bibliotheek*, 484.†
72. **Francisco del Tuppo:**
    a. Amsterdam, *Crevenna Sale*, 1789, 180 *fl.*
    b. Escorial, *R. Bibl. S. Laurentii Escurialensis*, j. v. N. 2.
    c. Hannover, *Kgl. Öffentliche Bibl.*, 54.

---

*Seen by Brunet; this is probably the same copy as that seen by Robert, cf. description of his work given on p. 2 of this *Manual*; see Vol. I, p. ccxlv.

† Seen by Hervieux.

‡ Seen by Hervieux; cf. also reference given for 37*k* (2.), p. 23, col. 1.

§ Cf. 1. *The Bibliographer's Manual of English Literature*, by William Thomas Lowndes. Vol. I. London: William Pickering, 1834. 8vo, xv and 482 pp. See p. 15, col. 1.

2. Ditto, second edition, revised by Henry G. Bohn. Vol. I. London: George Bell and Sons, York Street, Covent Garden, 1875. 12mo, 576 pp. See pp. 15–16.

3. Cf. reference given for 37*i.* See p. 17, No. 106 (and also No. 107).

4. *Early Illustrated Books: A History of the Decoration and Illustration of Books in the 15th and 16th Centuries*, by Alfred W. Pollard. London: Kegan Paul, Trench, Trübner (and) Co., Ltd., 1893. 8vo, xvi and 256 pp. See p. 225.

5. Cf. reference given for 35*c.* See pp. 15–16, No. 8, note. The woodcut of Æsop contained in this copy is said to be unique.

d. Heidelberg, *Universitätsbibl.*, Sch. 69. n. 450.
e. London, *Bernard Quaritch Cat.*, 1874, £80.*
f. London, *British Museum*, 167. f. 14.   Imperfect.
g. London, *British Museum*, G. 7807.
h. London, *Hibbert Sale*, 1829, £17.
i. London, *Pinelli Sale*, 1789, £12.
j. London, *Unspecified Sale*, 1816, £26 15s.
k. Oxford, *Bodleian Libr.*, Douce 225.
l. Paris, *Boutourlin Sale*, 1839–1841, 36 *fr.* 50 *c.* Imperfect.
m. Paris, *Brienne-Laire Sale*, 1791, 606 *fr.*
n. Paris, *Libri Sale*, 1847–1858, 480 *fr.*
o. Paris, *Unspecified Sale*, 1610 *fr.*
p. Wien, *K. u. K. Hofbibl.*, iv. F. 4.
q. Copy seen by Robert.†

73. **Hainricus Stainhöwel:**
   a. (No copy known to me.)
74. **Hainricus Stainhöwel:**
   a. London, *South Kensington Museum*, (?).‡   Imperfect.
75. **Hainricus Stainhöwel:**
   a. Darmstadt, *Grossherzogl. Hofbibl.*, (?).§
   b. Haag, *Kong. Bibliotheek*, 593.
76. **Bonus Accursius:**
   a. London, *British Museum*, G. 7718.
   b. London, *British Museum*, G. 7733.
77. **Gualterus Anglicus:**
   a. Paris, *Celotti Sale*, 1825, 81 *fr.*
78. **Hainricus Stainhöwel:**
   a. Basel, *Museum*, A. M. v. 6.‡
   b. Bern, *Bibl. Bongarsiana*, Inc. 42.‡

---

* Cf. reference given for 17*c.* See p. 355, No. 3730 ; this copy formerly belonged to M. Yéméniz.
† Cf. description of his work given on p. 2 of this *Manual.* See Vol. I, p. ccxlviii.
‡ Seen by Hervieux.
§ Cf. reference given for 35*b.* See p. 41, No. 25.

    c. Heidelberg, *Universitätsbibl.*, Sch. 69. n. 449.*
    d. London, *British Museum*, C. 19. d. 5.*
    e. Oxford, *Bodleian Libr.*, Auct. N. 4. 16.*
    f. Oxford, *Bodleian Libr.*, Auct. Q. 4. 30.*
    g. Oxford, *Bodleian Libr.*, Douce 226.*

79. **Gualterus Anglicus:**
    a. (No copy known to me.)

80. **Hainricus Stainhöwel:**
    a. Bruxelles, *Bibl. Royale*, 2486.*
    b. Cambridge, Eng., *University Libr.*, (?).†
    c. London, *British Museum*, G. 7808.
    d. Wien, *K. u. K. Hofbibl.*, iv. H. 3.

81. **Julien Macho:**
    a. Wien, *K. u. K. Hofbibl.*, x. G. 1.*

82. **Nicolaus Pergamenus:**
    a. London, *British Museum*, C. 38. h. 4.‡
    b. Paris, *Cailhava Sale*, 1845-1852, 199 *fr.*
    c. Paris, *Unspecified Sale*, 650 *fr.*

83. **Nicolaus Pergamenus:**
    a. (No copy known to me.)

84. **Vincentius Bellovacensis:**
    a. London, *Heber Sale*, 1834-1836, £1 13s.§
    b. Paris, *Bearzi Sale*, 1855, 190 *fr.*

85. **Accio Zuccho:**
    a. London, *British Museum*, C. 20. b. 12.
    b. Oxford, *Bodleian Libr.*, Douce 62.
    c. Paris, *Libri Sale*, 1847-1858, 175 *fr.*
    d. Sevilla, *Bibl. Colombina*, 4. 6. 16 (formerly C. FF. Tab. 169. N. 52).‖

---

* Seen by Hervieux.
† Seen by Hervieux; this copy was bought at London in 1875 for £31 10s.
‡ Cf. reference given for 35g. See col. 22.
§ Brunet states that this set, including No. 66 of the present list, consists of four volumes.
‖ Ferdinando Colombo has inscribed his name in this copy with the date 1537.

86. **Bonus Accursius:**
  a. London, *British Museum*, G. 7733.
87. **Gualterus Anglicus:**
  a. (No copy known to me.)
88. **Gualterus Anglicus:**
  a. (No copy known to me.)
89. **Hainricus Stainhöwel:**
  a. (No copy known to me.)
90. **Hainricus Stainhöwel:**
  a. Prag, *Strahöfer Bibl.*, (?).*
91. **Gualterus Anglicus:**
  a. Amsterdam, *Meermann Sale*, 30 fl.
  b. Bruxelles, *Bibl. Royale*, 1529 (formerly 997).
  c. London, *British Museum*, C. I. a. 4. Imperfect.
  d. London, *Hibbert Sale*, 1829, £2 5s.
  e. Oxford, *Bodleian Libr.*, Douce 60.
92. **Gualterus Anglicus:**
  a. (No copy known to me.)
93. **Nicolaus Pergamenus:**
  a. London, *British Museum*, 637. k. 16.†
94. **Hainricus Stainhöwel:**
  a. (No copy known to me.)
95. **Gualterus Anglicus:**
  a. London, *British Museum*, 12304. ee. 43.
  b. München, *Kgl. Hof- u. Staatsbibl.*, Inc. c. a. 620.
  c. Nürnberg, *Stadtbibl.*, 139.
  d. Wien, *K. u. K. Hofbibl.*, xvi. G. 29.
96. **Gualterus Anglicus:**
  a. Linz, *K. u. K. Studienbibl.*, B. 131. b.
  b. London, *British Museum*, 12305. e. 12.
  c. München, *Kgl. Hof- u. Staatsbibl.*, Inc. c. a. 621.
  d. St. Gallen, *Vadianische Bibl.*, 762.‡
  e. Wien, *K. u. K. Hofbibl.*, vii. H. 2.

---

* This copy consists merely of a fragment of two leaves, which is all that is extant of this edition according to Ebert; cf. reference given for 36e, col. 24, No. 261.

† Cf. reference given for 35g. See col. 22.

‡ Cf. reference given for 66e. See p. 142.

97. **Gualterus Anglicus:**
    a. Wien, *K. u. K. Hofbibl.*, x. H. 66.
98. **Hainricus Stainhöwel:**
    a. Escorial, *R. Bibl. S. Laurentii Escurialensis,* I. Z.
    13.*
99. **Hainricus Stainhöwel:**
    a. London, *Payne and Foss Cat.,* 1824, No. 1526.
100. **Accio Zuccho:**
    a. (No copy known to me.)
101. **Gualterus Anglicus:**
    a. Grenoble, *Bibl. Municipale,* 173.
    b. Würzburg, *Universitätsbibl.,* L. R. 9. 44.†
102. **Gualterus Anglicus:**
    a. Haag, *Kong. Bibliotheek,* 345.
    b. London, *British Museum,* 12305. e. 11.
    c. München, *Kgl. Hof- u. Staatsbibl.,* Inc. c. a. 716.
    d. Oxford, *Bodleian Libr.,* Auct. 5. Q. 6. 68.
    e. Stuttgart, *Kgl. Öffentliche Bibl.,* (?).
    f. Wien, *K. u. K. Hofbibl.,* xxvi. G. 32.
103. **Gualterus Anglicus:**
    a. London, *British Museum,* G. 7736.
    b. Oxford, *Bodleian Libr.,* A. q. q. Linc.‡
    c. Stuttgart, *Kgl. Öffentliche Bibl.,* (?).
104. **Gualterus Anglicus:**
    a. (No copy known to me.)
105. **Accio Zuccho:**
    a. Milano, *Bibl. Ambrosiana,* S. Q. R. II. 18.† Im-
    perfect.
    b. Milano, *Bibl. Nazionale di Brera,* AM. IX. 43.†
    Imperfect.
    c. Milano, *Bibl. Nazionale di Brera,* AN. X. 20.†
    Imperfect.

---

* Seen by Hervieux ; this is probably the same copy that was seen by
Amador de los Rios.
† Seen by Hervieux.
‡ Cf. reference given for 37*k.* (2.). See p. 23, col. 1.

106. **Gabrielis Bracii**:
   a. Paris, *Brienne-Laire Sale*, 1791, 42 *fr.*
107. **Gualterus Anglicus**:
   a. Bruxelles, *Bibl. Royale*, 74 (formerly 1358).*
   b. Dijon, *Bibl. Municipale*, 10974.
108. **Gualterus Anglicus**:
   a. (No copy known to me.)
109. **Gualterus Anglicus**:
   a. Bern, *Bibl. Bongarsiana*, Inc. 153.
110. **Gualterus Anglicus**:
   a. (No copy known to me.)
111. **Gualterus Anglicus**:
   a. London, *British Museum*, 12304. ee. 17.
112. **Guillaume Tardif**:
   a. London, *Bernard Quaritch Cat.*, 1888, £20.†
   b. Paris, *Bibl. Nationale*, (?).
   c. Paris, *La Vallière Sale*, 1767, 12 *fr.*
113. **Hainricus Stainhöwel**:
   a. Darmstadt, *Grossherzogl. Hofbibl.*, (?).‡
   b. Dresden, *Kgl. Öffentliche Bibl.*, (?).
114. **Julien Macho**:
   a. London. *British Museum*, 638. k. 2.
115. **Laurentius Valla**:
   a. London, *British Museum*, C. 1. a. 3.
116. **Vincentius Bellovacensis**:
   a. (No copy known to me.)
117. **Accio Zuccho**:
   a. London, *Beckford Sale*, 1882.§
   b. Venezia, *Bibl. Nazionale Marciana*, CXIII. 7. 41304.‖
   c. Wien, *K. u. K. Hofbibl.*, iv. H. 36.‖

* In his first volume Hervieux gave the shelf number as 229.
† Cf. reference given for 7*a.* (2.). See p. 60, No. 394 ; this copy has the name of Girardot de Préfond stamped in a straight line on the leather below the roulette inside the cover.
‡ Cf. reference given for 35*b.* See p. 41, No. 26.
§ Cf. reference given for 35*c.* See p. 6, No. 66.
‖ Seen by Hervieux.

118. **Gualterus Anglicus:**
    a. (No copy known to me.)
119. **Gualterus Anglicus:**
    a. Paris, *Hervieux' Libr.*, (?).
120. **Gualterus Anglicus:**
    a. (No copy known to me.)
121. **Hainricus Stainhöwel:**
    a. Carlsruhe, *Grossherzogl. Badische Hof- u. Landes-bibl.*, 22886. *2.*
122. **Nicolaus Pergamenus:**
    a. Darmstadt, *Grossherzogl. Hofbibl.*, (?).†
    b. London, *British Museum*, 1073. l. 2. (1.).‡
    c. Paris, *Regnault-Bretel Sale*, 1819, 18 *fr.*
123. **Gualterus Anglicus:**
    a. London, *British Museum*, G. 7724.
    b. Rouen, *Bibl. Municipale*, O. 638.
124. **Accio Zuccho:**
    a. Venezia, *Bibl. Nazionale Marciana*, CXIII. 7. 41304.§
    b. Wien, *K. u. K. Hofbibl.*, iv. H. 36.§
125. **Franciscus de Tuppo:**
    a. London, *Hibbert Sale*, 1829, £4 4s.
126. **Gualterus Anglicus:**
    a. Bruxelles, *Bibl. Royale*, 1840 (formerly 1620).
127. **Gualterus Anglicus:**
    a. Bruxelles, *Bibl. Royale*, 1740.
    b. London, *British Museum*, 1073. l. 28.‖
    c. London, *British Museum*, 12304. cc. 19. (3.).
    d. München, *Kgl. Hof- u. Staatsbibl.*, A. Lat. a. 13. g.

---

* Cf. note 1 on p. 28 of this *Manual.*
† Cf. reference given for 35*b*. See p. 42, No. 35.
‡ Cf. reference given for 35*g*. See col. 22.
§ Seen by Hervieux.
‖ Hervieux gives in each of his references a different shelf number for the single *British Museum* copy known to him; neither of them agrees with that given by the printed catalogue. Hervieux' numbers are : 1073. l. 1. (2.), and 1073. l. 28. (2.).

e. München, *Kgl. Hof- u. Staatsbibl.*, Inc. c. a. 870.
f. Oxford, *Bodleian Libr.*, Auct. 5. Q. 6. 80.
g. Padova, *R. Bibl. Universitaria*, So. XV. 496.
h. Wien, *K. u. K. Hofbibl.*, ix. H. 34.
i. Wolfenbüttel, *Herzogliche Bibl.*, Aus. 171. 14. Qu.
128. **Laurentius Valla :**
   a. (Same as preceding—an oversight.)
129. **Omnibonus Leonicenus :**
   a. London, *British Museum*, G. 7734.
130. **Laurentius Valla :**
   a. London, *British Museum*, 1073. l. 1.
   b. London, *British Museum*, 12304. cc. 19. (2.).
131. **Accio Zuccho :**
   a. London, *Beckford Sale*, 1882.*
   b. Verona, *Bibl. Comunale*, 77. 2.
132. **Franciscus de Tuppo :**
   a. München, *Kgl. Hof- u. Staatsbibl.*, Inc. c. a. 2800.
   b. Sevilla, *Bibl. Colombina*, 2. 6. 26 (formerly C. K.
    K. Tab. 196. N. 19).
133. **Francisco del Tuppo :**
   a. London, *Bernard Quaritch Cat.*, 1888, £250.†
134. **Francisco del Tuppo :**
   a. London, *British Museum*, G. 7735.
   b. Oxford, *Bodleian Libr.*; (?).‡
135. **Avianus :**
   a. Köln, *Stadtbibl.*, C. B. II. c. 257. f.
   b. London, *British Museum*, 1073. l. 33.
136. **Gualterus Anglicus :**
   a. Nevers, *Bibl. Municipale*, 28.
137. **Gualterus Anglicus :**
   a. Dijon, *Bibl. Municipale*, 10973.

---

* Cf. reference given for 35*c.* See p. 6, No. 76.
† Cf. 1. Reference given for 7*a.* (2.). See p. 20, No. 119 ; this copy bears the inscription : " Io. Grolieri et amicorum."
2. Reference given for 25*a.* (2.). See p. 84, No. 1150 ; in this later catalogue the price has been advanced to £320.
‡ Cf. reference given for 37*k.* (2.). See p. 23, col. 1.

138. **Gualterus Anglicus :**
    a. Linz, *K. u. K. Studienbibl.*, B. 100. B.
    b. London, *British Museum*, G. 7738.
    c. München, *Kgl. Hof- u. Staatsbibl.*, Inc. c. a. 1054.
    d. München, *Kgl. Hof- u. Staatsbibl.*, A. Gr. b. 59.
    e. München, *Kgl. Hof- u. Staatsbibl.*, A. Gr. b. 60.
    f. München, *Kgl. Hof- u. Staatsbibl.*, A. Gr. b. 536.
139. **Gualterus Anglicus :**
    a. Haag, *Kong. Bibliotheek*, 364.
    b. Linz, *K. u. K. Studienbibl.*, B. 73.
    c. Paris, *Unspecified Sale*, 25 *fr.*
140. **Vincentius Bellovacensis :**
    a. London, *British Museum*, 526. n. 4.*
    b. London, *Thorold Sale*, 1884.†
    c. St. Gallen, *Vadianische Bibl.*, 786.‡
    d. Venezia, *Bibl. Monasterii S. Michaelis Venetiarum
        Prope Murianum*, (?).§
    e. Washington, *Libr. of Congress*, (?).‖
141. **Vincentius Bellovacensis :**
    a. London, *British Museum*, 1309. 1.¶

---

* Cf. *British Museum : Catalogue of Printed Books*. Victoria-Virgilius.
London : printed by William Clowes and Sons, limited, Stamford Street
and Charing Cross, 1890. fo, 446 cols. See col. 356.
  † Cf. reference given for 8*b.* See p. 187, No. 2043.
  ‡ Cf. reference given for 66*c.* See p. 345.
  § Cf. *Bibliotheca Codicum Manuscriptorum Monasterii S. Michaelis
Venetiarum Prope Murianum, una cum Appendice Librorum Impres-
sorum Seculi XV.* Opus posthumum Johannis-Benedicti Mittarelli,
Veneti Abbatis Ex-Generalis Benedictino-Camaldulensis. Venetiis,
1779. Ex Typographia Fentiana : sumptibus Præfati Monasterii. fo,
xxiv pp. and 1257 cols. ; viii and xv pp.; 491 cols. See *Seculi XV.
Appendix Librorum*, col. 475.
  ‖ Cf. *Catalogue of the Books Added to the Library of Congress from
December* 1, 1866, *to December* 1, 1867. Washington : Government
Printing Office, 1868. 4to, ii and 526 pp. See p. 437, col. 1.
  On April 7, 1896, an unsuccessful attempt was made by me to verify
this entry ; the overcrowding of the library has resulted in many books
being " unfindable."
  ¶ Cf. reference given for 140*a.* See col. 356.

b. Paris, *Hervieux' Libr.*, (?).

c. Venezia, *Bibl. Monasterii S. Michaelis Venetiarum Prope Murianum*, (?).*

142. **Gualterus Anglicus:**
    a. Oxford, *Bodleian Libr.*, Douce 58.

143. **Jehan de Vignay:**
    a. London, *British Museum*, 580. k. 1.†
    b. London, *British Museum*, C. 22. d.† Imperfect.
    c. Paris, *Bibl. de Sainte-Geneviève*, (?).‡
    d. Paris, *Bibl. Nationale*, G. 203–207.§

144. **Laurentius Abstemius:**
    a. Copy seen by Robert.‖

145. **Gualterus Anglicus:**
    a. (No copy known to me.)

146. **Gualterus Anglicus:**
    a. London, *British Museum*, 12304. ee. 41.

147. **Gualterus Anglicus:**
    a. London, *British Museum*, G. 7723.

148. **Julien Macho:**
    a. London, *British Museum*, G. 7806.

149. **Laurentius Valla:**
    a. London, *British Museum*, G. 7719.

150. **Gualterus Anglicus:**
    a. London, *British Museum*, 1073, l. 29.¶

151. **Gualterus Anglicus:**
    a. Milano, *Bibl. Nazionale di Brera*, AM. X. 7.§

152. **Gualterus Anglicus:**
    a. Arras, *Bibl. Municipale*, 14680.

---

* Cf. reference given for 140*d.* See col. 475.
† Cf. reference given for 140*a.* See col. 356.
‡ Brunet states that this edition consists of five volumes.
§ Seen by Hervieux.
‖ Cf. description of his work given on p. 2 of this *Manual.* See Vol. I, p. ccxli.

¶ Hervieux gives in each of his references a different shelf number for this copy; neither of them agrees with that given by the printed catalogue. Hervieux' numbers are: 1073. l. 1. 2.*, and 1073. l. 29. 2*.

153. **Gualterus Anglicus** :
     a. (No copy known to me.)
154. **Gualterus Anglicus** :
     a. Firenze, *R. Bibl. Riccardiana*, 560.*
155. **Hainricus Stainhöwel** :
     a. (No copy known to me.)
156. **Hainricus Stainhöwel** :
     a. Paris, *Bibl. Nationale*, (?).†
157. **Accio Zuccho** :
     a. Carpentras, *Bibl. Municipale*, E. 1320.
     b. Ferrara, *Bibl. Comunale*, O. 66.
     c. London, *British Museum*, C. 20. b.
     d. London, *Heber Sale*, 1834–1836, £2 19*s*.
     e. Oxford, *Bodleian Libr.*, Auct. 6. Q. 6. 74.
     f. Paris, *Unspecified Sale*, 170 *fr.*
158. **Accio Zuccho** :
     a. London, *Sunderland Sale*, 1881.‡
159. **Bonus Accursius** :
     a. Amsterdam, *Crevenna Sale*, 1789, 25 *fl.*
     b. Amsterdam, *Meermann Sale*, 41 *fl.*
     c. London, *British Museum*, C. 1. a. 1. (2.).
     d. London, *British Museum*, C. 19. c. (2.).
     e. London, *British Museum*, G. 7726. (1.).
     f. London, *Gennadius Sale*, 1895, (?).§

---

* Cf. reference given for 36*a*. See pp. clxxvii–clxxx.

† Seen by Morel-Fatio ; this was probably the copy that was seen by Robert ; cf. description of his work given on p. 2 of this *Manual.* See Vol. I, p. ccxlviii.

‡ Cf. *Sale Catalogue of the Sunderland or Blenheim Library: Portion the First;* to be sold by auction by Messrs. Puttick and Simpson, 47 Leicester Square, London, W. C., 1881. 8vo, viii and 213 pp. See p. 8.

§ This copy formerly belonged to Mr. Lakelands ; cf. *Catalogue of the Extensive and Valuable Library of Manuscripts* (and) *Printed Books of his Excellency Monsieur John Gennadius, D.C.L., F.R.S.L., Late Greek Minister at the Court of St. James's,* which will be sold by auction by Messrs. Sotheby, Wilkinson (and) Hodge at their house, No. 13 Wellington Street, Strand, W. C. (London), 1895. 8vo, xv and 283 pp. See p. 5.

g. London, *Hibbert Sale,* 1829, £3 13s.

h. London, *Hibbert Sale (bis),* 1829, £3 15s.

i. Oxford, *Bodleian Libr.,* (?).*

j Paris, *Reine Sale,* 1834–1840, 41 *fr.*

160. **Gualterus Anglicus:**
    a. Linz, *K. u. K. Studienbibl.,* B. 111.
    b. London, *British Museum,* 12304. ee. 42.
    c. München, *Kgl. Hof- u. Staatsbibl.,* Inc. c. a. 1360.
    d. München, *Kgl. Hof- u. Staatsbibl.,* A. Gr. b. 61.
    e. Oxford, *Bodleian Libr.,* Auct. Q. 5. 53.
    f. Stuttgart, *Kgl. Öffentliche Bibl.,* (?).
    g. Wien, *K. u. K. Hofbibl.,* x. H. 47.

161. **Gualterus Anglicus:**
    a. London, *British Museum,* 12304. e. 5.
    b. Paris, *Costabili Sale,* 45 *fr.*
    c. Verona, *Bibl. Comunale,* 79. e.

162. **Gualterus Anglicus:**
    a. (No copy known to me.)

163. **Sebastianus Brandt:**
    a. (No copy known to me.)

164. **Accio Zuccho:**
    a. London, *British Museum,* 1073. l. 26.
    b. Milano, *Bibl. Ambrosiana,* S. Q. Q. II. 18.
    c. Milano, *Bibl. Nazionale di Brera,* AM. IX. 43.
    d. Milano, *Bibl. Nazionale di Brera,* AN. X. 20.
    e. Padova, *R. Bibl. Universitaria,* So. XV. 494.

165. **Gabrielis Bracii:**
    a. Althorp, *Earl Spencer's Libr.,* (?).†
    b. London, *British Museum,* 1067. m. 6.
    c. London, *British Museum,* G. 7717.
    d. London, *Pinelli Sale,* 1789, £40 19s.
    e. London, *Sunderland Sale,* 1881.†
    f. London, *Thorold Sale,* 1884.‡

---

* Cf. reference given for 37*k.* (2.). See p. 23, col. 1.
† Cf. reference given for 158*a.* See p. 7.
‡ Cf. reference given for 8*b.* See p. 5, No. 38.

    g. Manchester, *Mrs. Rylands' Libr.*, (?).*

    h. Oxford, *Bodleian Libr.*, (?).†

    i. Paris, *Brienne-Laire Sale*, 1791, 200 *fr.*

166. **Gualterus Anglicus:**

    a. (No copy known to me.)

167. **Gualterus Anglicus:**

    a. Basel, *Museum*, C. E. VI. 49.

168. **Gualterus Anglicus:**

    a. Oxford, *Bodleian Libr.*, (?).

169. **Hainricus Stainhöwel:**

    a. London, *Bernard Quaritch Cat.*, 1886, £5.‡

170. **Hainricus Stainhöwel:**

    a. Gand, *Bibl. de la Ville et de l'Univ.*, Rés. 35.

    b. London, *British Museum*, C. 20. e.

    c. Copy seen by Robert.§

171. **Gualterus Anglicus:**

    a. Bruxelles, *Bibl. Royale*, 2075 (formerly 2044).

172. **Julien Macho:**

    a. London, *British Museum*, 638. k. 2.‖

    b. Paris, *Coulon Sale*, 1829, 175 *fr.* Imperfect.

173. **Laurentius Abstemius:**

    a. Copy seen by Robert.¶

174. **Bonus Accursius:**

    a. Carlsruhe, *Grossherzogl. Badische Hof- u. Landes-Bibl.*, 22886. 31.**

175. **Gualterus Anglicus:**

    a. Basel, *Museum*, D. D. VII. 12.

    b. Hannover, *Kgl. Öffentliche Bibl.*, 201.

---

* 165*a* and 165*g* are identical. Earl Spencer's Library was removed to Manchester in 1893.

† Cf. reference given for 37*k.* (2.). See p. 23, col. 1.

‡ Cf. reference given for 7*a.* See p. 3560, No. 36076.

§ Cf. description of his work given on p. 2 of this *Manual.* See Vol. I, p. ccxliii.

‖ In his fourth volume, p. 409, Hervieux gives this reference as being to a copy of No. 114 of this list.

¶ Cf. description of his work given on p. 2 of this *Manual.* See Vol. I, p. ccxli.

** Cf. note 1 on p. 28 of this *Manual.*

176. **Gualterus Anglicus:**
    a. (No copy known to me.)
177. **Nicolaus Pergamenus:**
    a. Darmstadt, *Grossherzogl. Hofbibl.*, (?).*
    b. Paris, *Salle Silvestre*, 1842, 21 *fr.*
178. **William Caxton:**
    a. London, *British Museum*, C. 38. g. 2. Imperfect.
    b. London, *British Museum*, 12305. g.
    c. London, *John Radcliffe's Libr.*, (?).†

REFERENCE LISTS.

a. *Authors.*

1. **Abstemius,** see Nos. 144, 173.
2. **Accursius,** see Nos. 11, 19, 21, 26, 31, 37, 60, 76, 86, 159, 174.
3. **Avianus,** see Nos. 16, 135.
4. **Boner,** see Nos. 1, 2.
5. **Bracii,** see Nos. 106, 165.
6. **Brandt,** see No. 163.
7. **Caxton,** see Nos. 70, 178.
8. **Gualterus,** see Nos. 8, 14, 15, 18, 20, 22, 27, 28, 33, 48, 49, 50, 55, 77, 79, 87, 88, 91, 92, 95, 96, 97, 101, 102, 103, 104, 107, 108, 109, 110, 111, 118, 119, 120, 123, 126, 127, 136, 137, 138, 139, 142, 145, 146, 147, 150, 151, 152, 153, 154, 160, 161, 162, 166, 167, 168, 171, 175, 176.
9. **Macho,** see Nos. 30, 34, 57, 67, 81, 114, 148, 172.
10. **Mansion,** see Nos. 54, 62.
11. **Nicolaus,** see Nos. 35, 51, 52, 53, 58, 59, 65, 82, 83, 93, 122, 177.

---

* Cf. reference given for 35*b*. See p. 44, No. 57.
† Cf. *A View of the English Editions, Translations and Illustrations of the Ancient Greek and Latin Authors*, with remarks, by Lewis William Brüggemann. Stettin: printed by Iohn Samuel Leich, 1797. 8vo, xvi and 838 pp. See p. 50.

12. **Omnibonus,** see Nos. 6, 129.
13. **Philelphus,** see No. 32.
14. **Remicius,** see No. 7.
15. **Stainhöwel,** see Nos. 17, 38, 39, 40, 41, 42, 43, 44,
    56, 64, 71, 73, 74, 75, 78, 80, 89, 90, 94, 98, 99, 113,
    121, 155, 156, 169, 170.
16. **Tardif,** see No. 112.
17. **Tuppo,** see Nos. 63, 72, 125, 132, 133, 134.
18. **Valla,** see Nos. 3, 24, 115, 128, 130, 149.
19. **Vignay,** see Nos. 29, 143.
20. **Vincentius,** see Nos. 4, 5, 9, 10, 12, 13, 45, 46, 66, 68,
    69, 84, 116, 140, 141.
21. **Zuccho,** see Nos. 23, 25, 36, 47, 61, 85, 100, 105, 117,
    124, 131, 157, 158, 164.

*b. Cities Where Printed.**

1. **Anonymous,** see Nos. 2, 3, 6, 14, 18, 21, 22, 23, 24,
   30, 36, 37, 38, 39, 40, 41, 42, 43, 44, 45, 46, 57, 71,
   76, 77, 78, 88, 91, 95, 96, 102, 105, 106, 107, 108, 109,
   110, 111, 113, 116, 119, 123, 126, 127, 128, 129, 135,
   138, 146, 147, 148, 160, 161, 162, 163, 168, 176, 177,
   178.
2. **Antwerp,** see Nos. 75, 80, 82, 87, 91 (?), 118, 122, 130.
3. **Aquileja,** see Nos. 63, 132, 133.
4. **Augsburg,** see Nos. 7, 12, 38 (?), 39 (?), 40 (?), 41 (?),
   42 (?), 43 (?), 44 (?), 64, 71 (?), 73, 89, 121, 155, 169.
5. **Bamberg,** see Nos. 1, 2 (?).
6. **Bologna,** see No. 79.
7. **Brescia,** see Nos. 48, 85, 97, 129 (?), 161.
8. **Burgos,** see No. 156.
9. **Cologne,** see Nos. 9n, 14 (?), 52, 104, 135n, 160.
10. **Delft,** see Nos. 93, 170.
11. **Deventer,** see Nos. 102 (?), 103, 115, 128 (?), 135 (?),
    139, 142, 145, 149, 150, 153, 166, 175.

---

* For a list of the Latin names of cities mentioned, with their English
equivalents, see p. 10, note 1.

12. **Engolisme**, see No. 120.
13. **Florence**, see Nos. 154, 174.
14. **Geneva**, see No. 177 (?).
15. **Gouda**, see Nos. 35, 51, 53, 54, 56, 58, 59, 74, 83.
16. **Haguenau**, see No. 138 (?).
17. **London**, see Nos. 70, 116 (?), 178 (?).
18. **Lyons**, see Nos. 29, 30 (?), 33, 34, 57 (?), 62, 67, 81, 92,
    101, 114, 136, 137, 152, 167, 168 (?), 172.
19. **Mayence**, see No. 163 (?).
20. **Milan**, see Nos. 11, 19, 22 (?), 26, 31, 37 (?), 60, 105 (?),
    151, 158, 164.
21. **Modena**, see No. 50.
22. **Mondovi**, see Nos. 20, 49.
23. **Naples**, see No. 72.
24. **Nuremberg**, see Nos. 66, 84.
25. **Paris**, see Nos. 13, 94, 108 (?), 111 (?), 112, 123 (?), 143,
    147 (?), 171.
26. **Prague**, see No. 90.
27. **Reggio**, see No. 159.
28. **Rome**, see Nos. 8, 15, 21 (?), 61, 76 (?), 86.
29. **Saragossa**, see No. 98.
30. **Stockholm**, see No. 65.
31. **Strasbourg**, see Nos. 4, 5, 9, 10, 28, 45 (?), 46 (?), 78 (?).
32. **Toscolano**, see No. 27.
33. **Toulouse**, see No. 99.
34. **Ulm**, see Nos. 16, 17.
35. **Venice**, see Nos. 6 (?), 32, 47, 55, 68, 69, 100, 117, 124,
    125, 131, 134, 140, 141, 144, 157, 165, 173.
36. **Verona**, see No. 25.

c. *Printers.*

1. **Aleman**, see No. 156.
2. **Alvise**, see No. 25.
3. **Anonymous**, see Nos. 2, 3, 6, 7, 12, 13, 14, 18, 21, 22,
   23, 24, 30, 36, 37, 38, 39, 40, 41, 42, 43, 44, 45, 46,

48, 55, 57, 61, 68, 69, 71, 72, 76, 77, 78, 87, 88, 93,
95, 96, 99, 102, 105, 106, 107, 108, 109, 110, 111, 113,
119, 120, 123, 127, 128, 135, 136, 138, 146, 147, 148,
155, 160, 162, 163, 165, 167, 168, 174, 176, 177.

4. **Bac.**, see No. 130.
5. **Bellot**, see No. 177 (?).
6. **Bertochus**, see No. 159.
7. **Bocard**, see No. 147 (?).
8. **Bonaccorsi**, see Nos. 60, 154.
9. **Boninis, de**, see Nos. 85, 97.
10. **Breda, de**, see Nos. 102 (?), 103, 115, 128 (?), 135 (?), 139, 142, 149, 150, 166, 175.
11. **Buyer**, see No. 29.
12. **C., M.**, see No. 32.
13. **Caxton**, see Nos. 70, 116.
14. **Cereto, de**, see Nos. 144, 173.
15. **Chaussard**, see Nos. 114, 152, 172.
16. **Conradus**, see No. 52.
17. **Eckert**, see No. 170.
18. **Fabri**, see Nos. 33, 101.
19. **Fabro, de**, see No. 92n.
20. **Farfengo**, see No. 129.
21. **Flachen**, see No. 28.
22. **Franciscus**, see No. 50.
23. **Franck**, see Nos. 61 (?), 76 (?), 86.
24. **Gran**, see No. 138 (?).
25. **Guldenschaf**, see No. 14 (?).
26. **Guldinbeck**, see No. 21 (?).
27. **Hamell, de**, see Nos. 63, 132, 133.
28. **Hurus**, see No. 98.
29. **Husz**, see Nos. 30n, 57 (?), 62, 67, 81, 137.
30. **Knoblotzer**, see No. 78 (?).
31. **Koburger**, see Nos. 66, 84.
32. **Lambillon**, see No. 126.
33. **Lavagnia**, see Nos. 26, 31.
34. **Leeu**, see Nos. 35, 51, 53, 54, 56, 58, 59, 74, 75, 80, 82, 83, 91, 118, 122.

35. **Levet**, see Nos. 94, 171.
36. **Liechtenstein**, see Nos. 140, 141.
37. **Lupi**, see Nos. 167 (?), 168 (?).
38. **Mantegatiis, de**, see No. 151.
39. **Mareschal**, see Nos. 114, 152, 172.
40. **Masson, de**, see Nos. 63, 132, 133.
41. **Mentellin**, see Nos. 4, 5, 9, 10, 45, 46 (?).
42. **Misuitis, de**, see No. 161.
43. **Monteferato, de**, see Nos. 47, 100, 117, 124, 125, 131, 134, 157.
44. **Moravo**, see No. 72 (?).
45. **Pafroed**, see Nos. 145, 153.
46. **Pteri**, see No. 27.
47. **Pfister**, see Nos. 1, 2 (?).
48. **Philippi, Ioannes**, see No. 8.
49. **Philippi, Nicholas**, see Nos. 30, 34, 57n.
50. **Pontanus**, see No. 3 (?).
51. **Prato, de**, see No. 92.
52. **Pynson**, see No. 178.
53. **Quentel**, see Nos. 104, 135n, 60 (?).
54. **Ratdolt**, see No. 71 (?).
55. **Reinhardi**, see Nos. 30, 34, 57n.
56. **Rugerius**, see No. 79.
57. **Schabeller**, see Nos. 30n, 57 (?), 62, 67.
58. **Schobsser**, see Nos. 73, 89.
59. **Schöffer**, see No. 163 (?).
60. **Schönsperger**, see Nos. 121, 155 (?), 169.
61. **Scinzenzeler**, see No. 158.
62. **Septemcastrensis**, see No. 50.
63. **Signerre, le**, see Nos. 105 (?), 164.
64. **Silber**, see Nos. 61 (?), 76 (?), 86.
65. **Snell**, see No. 65.
66. **Sorg**, see Nos. 12 (?), 38 (?), 39 (?), 40 (?), 41 (?), 42 (?), 43 (?), 64.
67. **Stella, de**, see Nos. 63, 132, 133.
68. **Valdarfer**, see No. 6 (?).

69. **Verard,** see Nos. 112, 143.
70. **Vivaldis, de,** see Nos. 20, 49.
71. **Willa, de,** see No. 15.
72. **Zainer, Guentherus,** see No. 44 (?).
73. **Zainer, Johannes,** see Nos. 16, 17.
74. **Zarotus,** see Nos. 11, 19.

d. Size of the Folio Editions.

1. **30 leaves,** see No. 49.
2. **36 leaves,** see No. 112.
3. **62 leaves,** see No. 52.
4. **72 leaves,** see Nos. 30, 47n, 57, 117n, 148n.
5. **74 leaves,** see No. 82.
6. **75 leaves,** see No. 163.
7. **77 leaves,** see No. 2.
8. **88 leaves,** see Nos. 1, 148.
9. **94 leaves,** see No. 178.
10. **100 leaves,** see No. 170.
11. **101 leaves,** see No. 54.
12. **102 leaves,** see Nos. 54n, 156.
13. **103 leaves,** see Nos. 35, 51, 58.
14. **104 leaves,** see No. 80.
15. **105 leaves,** see No. 169.
16. **112 leaves,** see No. 75.
17. **114 leaves,** see Nos. 71, 78.
18. **115 leaves,** see No. 43.
19. **120 leaves,** see No. 98.
20. **123 leaves,** see No. 63.
21. **125 leaves,** see No. 53.
22. **129 leaves,** see Nos. 38, 39.
23. **130 leaves,** see No. 38n.
24. **142 leaves,** see No. 70.
25. **146 leaves,** see No. 34.
26. **151 leaves,** see No. 121.
27. **155 leaves,** see Nos. 5, 15.
28. **158 leaves,** see No. 40.

29. **159 leaves,** see No. 133.
30. **167 leaves,** see No. 44.
31. **168 leaves,** see Nos. 10, 72, 132.
32. **170 leaves,** see No. 42.
33. **180 leaves,** see No. 113.
34. **190 leaves,** see No. 41.
35. **196 leaves,** see No. 64.
36. **255 leaves,** see No. 140.
37. **275 leaves,** see No. 17n.
38. **288 leaves,** see No. 17.
39. **326 leaves,** see No. 12.
40. **332 leaves,** see No. 143.
41. **336 leaves,** see No. 12n.
42. **400 leaves,** see Nos. 4, 9.
43. **Unspecified,** see Nos. 7, 13, 16, 20, 45, 46, 59, 62, 66, 67, 73, 81n, 83, 84, 89, 93, 99, 141, 155, 177.

e. Size of the Quarto Editions.

1. **6 leaves,** see Nos. 115, 130, 149.
2. **18 leaves,** see Nos. 79, 151.
3. **19 leaves,** see Nos. 22, 86.
4. **20 leaves,** see Nos. 15, 77, 110.
5. **22 leaves,** see No. 129.
6. **24 leaves,** see Nos. 3, 32.
7. **26 leaves,** see No. 135n.
8. **28 leaves,** see No. 173.
9. **29 leaves,** see No. 144.
10. **30 leaves,** see No. 135.
11. **31 leaves,** see Nos. 103, 146.
12. **32 leaves,** see No. 96n.
13. **33 leaves,** see No. 96.
14. **34 leaves,** see No. 91.
15. **35 leaves,** see Nos. 108, 147.
16. **36 leaves,** see Nos. 127, 128, 138, 161, 171.
17. **37 leaves,** see No. 145.
18. **38 leaves,** see Nos. 60, 102, 107, 150, 159.

19. **39 leaves**, see Nos. 139, 160n.
20. **40 leaves**, see Nos. 111, 158, 160, 175.
21. **42 leaves**, see Nos. 6, 95, 123.
22. **44 leaves**, see No. 76.
23. **48 leaves**, see No. 165.
24. **50 leaves**, see Nos. 11, 26, 31.
25. **55 leaves**, see No. 19.
26. **56 leaves**, see No. 109.
27. **62 leaves**, see No. 14.
28. **63 leaves**, see No. 18.
29. **66 leaves**, see No. 21.
30. **70 leaves**, see No. 164.
31. **71 leaves**, see Nos. 100, 157n.
32. **72 leaves**, see Nos. 47, 117, 124, 131, 157.
33. **77 leaves**, see Nos. 114, 172.
34. **82 leaves**, see No. 61.
35. **92 leaves**, see No. 176.
36. **100 leaves**, see No. 85.
37. **120 leaves**, see No. 25.
38. **160 leaves**, see No. 25n.
39. **167 leaves**, see No. 37.
40. **186 leaves**, see No. 167.
41. **212 leaves**, see No. 136.
42. **286 leaves**, see Nos. 33, 101.
43. **Unspecified**, see Nos. 8, 23, 24, 27, 28, 29, 36, 48, 50,
    56, 65, 74, 81, 87, 88, 90, 92, 94, 97, 104, 105, 106,
    119, 120, 122, 125, 126, 134, 142, 152, 153, 162, 168.
44. **Unidentified**, see Nos. 55, 68, 69, 116, 118, 137, 154,
    166, 174.

f. Languages.

1. **Bohemian**, see No. 90.
2. **English**, see Nos. 70, 116, 178.
3. **Flemish**, see Nos. 53, 59, 74, 75, 83, 93, 170.
4. **French**, see Nos. 29, 30, 34, 54, 57, 62, 67, 81, 112,
   114, 143, 148, 172.

5. **German,** see Nos. 1, 2, 16, 17, 40, 41, 42, 43, 44, 64,
   73, 89, 113, 121, 155, 169.
6. **Greek,** see Nos. 37, 60, 106, 159, 165, 174.
7. **Italian,** see Nos. 23, 25, 36, 47, 55, 61, 63, 72, 85, 100,
   105, 117, 124, 125, 131, 132, 133, 134, 154, 157, 158,
   161, 164.
8. **Latin,** see Nos. 3, 4, 5, 6, 7, 8, 9, 10, 11, 12, 13, 14, 15,
   16, 17, 18, 19, 20, 21, 22, 23, 24, 25, 26, 27, 28, 31,
   32, 33, 35, 36, 37, 38, 39, 45, 46, 47, 48, 49, 50, 51,
   52, 55, 56, 58, 60, 61, 63, 65, 66, 68, 69, 71, 72, 76,
   77, 78, 79, 80, 82, 84, 85, 86, 87, 88, 91, 92, 94, 95,
   96, 97, 100, 101, 102, 103, 104, 105, 106, 107, 108,
   109, 110, 111, 115, 117, 118, 119, 120, 122, 123, 124,
   125, 126, 127, 128, 129, 130, 131, 132, 133, 134, 135,
   136, 137, 138, 139, 140, 141, 142, 144, 145, 146, 147,
   149, 150, 151, 152, 153, 157, 158, 159, 160, 161, 162,
   163, 164, 166, 167, 168, 171, 173, 174, 175, 176, 177.
9. **Spanish,** see Nos. 98, 99, 156.

g. *Cities Where Preserved.*

1. **Althorp:**
   a. Earl Spencer's Libr., see Nos. 17a, 37a, 165a.
2. **Amsterdam:**
   a. Crevenna Sale, see Nos. 72a, 159a.
   b. Enschedé Sale, see No. 3a.
   c. Meermann Sale, see Nos. 35a, 91a, 159b.
3. **Arras:**
   a. Bibl. Municipale, see No. 152a.
4. **Baltimore:**
   a. Johns Hopkins Univ. Libr., see No. 64a.
5. **Basel:**
   a. Museum, see Nos. 71a, 78a, 167a, 175a.
6. **Berlin:**
   a. Königliche Bibl., see No. 2a.
7. **Bern:**
   a. Bibl. Bongarsiana, see Nos. 78b, 109a.

8. **Boston** :
    a. Boston Public Libr., see Nos. 9*a*, 12*a*, 12*b*.
9. **Bruxelles** :
    a. Bibl. Royale, see Nos. 80*a*, 91*b*, 107*a*, 126*a*, 127*a*,
    171*a*.
10. **Cambridge, Eng.** :
    a. University Libr., see No. 80*b*.
11. **Carlsruhe** :
    a. Grossherzogl. Badische Hof- u. Landesbibl., see
    Nos. 121*a*, 174*a*.
12. **Carpentras** :
    a. Bibl. Municipale, see No. 157*a*.
13. **Darmstadt** :
    a. Grossherzogliche Hofbibl., see Nos. 35*b*, 59*a*, 75*a*,
    113*a*, 122*a*, 177*a*.
14. **Dijon** :
    a. Bibl. Municipale, see Nos. 107*b*, 137*a*.
15. **Dresden** :
    a. Kgl. Öffentliche Bibl., see No. 113*b*.
16. **Escorial** :
    a. R. Bibl. S. Laurentii Escurialensis, see Nos. 72*b*,
    98*a*.
17. **Ferrara** :
    a. Bibl. Comunale, see No. 157*b*.
18. **Firenze** :
    a. R. Bibl. Mediceo-Laurenziana, see Nos. 17*b*, 39*a*.
    b. R. Bibl. Nazionale Centrale, see No. 36*a*.
    c. R. Bibl. Riccardiana, see No. 154*a*.
19. **Gand** :
    a. Bibl. de la Ville et de l' Univ., see No. 170*a*.
20. **Grenoble** :
    a. Bibl. Municipale, see Nos. 33*a*, 101*a*.
21. **Haag** :
    a. Kong. Bibliotheek, see Nos. 75*b*, 102*a*, 139*a*.
    b. Martinus Nijhoff Cat., see No. 53*a*.
22. **Haarlem** :
    a. Städtische Bibl., see No. 3*b*.

23. **Hannover**:
    a. *Kgl. Öffentliche Bibl.*, see Nos. 72*c*, 175*b*.
24. **Heidelberg**:
    a. *Universitätsbibl.*, see Nos. 72*d*, 78*c*.
25. **Köln**:
    a. *Stadtbibl.*, see Nos. 54*a*, 135*a*.
26. **Linz**:
    a. *K. u. K. Studienbibl.*, see Nos. 39*b*, 64*b*, 96*a*, 138*a*, 139*b*, 160*a*.
27. **London**:
    a. *Beckford Sale*, see Nos. 35*c*, 117*a*, 131*a*.
    b. *Bernard Quaritch Cat.*, see Nos. 7*a*, 17*c*, 25*a*, 35*d*, 35*e*, 35*f*, 53*b*, 72*c*, 112*a*, 133*a*, 169*a*.
    c. *British Museum*, see Nos. 3*c*, 6*a*, 11*a*, 11*b*, 11*c*, 19*a*, 21*a*, 24*a*, 25*b*, 25*c*, 25*d*, 30*a*, 31*a*, 35*g*, 35*h*, 37*b*, 37*c*, 37*d*, 39*c*, 51*a*, 52*a*, 52*b*, 57*a*, 58*a*, 58*b*, 60*a*, 60*b*, 60*c*, 61*a*, 63*a*, 70*a*, 71*a*, 71*b*, 72*f*, 72*g*, 76*a*, 76*b*, 78*d*, 80*c*, 82*a*, 85*a*, 86*a*, 91*c*, 93*a*, 95*a*, 96*b*, 102*b*, 103*a*, 111*a*, 114*a*, 115*a*, 122*b*, 123*a*, 127*b*, 127*c*, 129*a*, 130*a*, 130*b*, 134*a*, 135*b*, 138*b*, 140*a*, 141*a*, 143*a*, 143*b*, 146*a*, 147*a*, 148*a*, 149*a*, 150*a*, 157*c*, 159*c*, 159*d*, 159*e*, 160*b*, 161*a*, 164*a*, 165*b*, 165*c*, 170*b*, 172*a*, 178*a*, 178*b*.
    d. *Cassano Serra Sale*, see No. 36*c*.
    e. *Duke of Devonshire's Libr.*, see No. 37*c*.
    f. *Gennadius Sale*, see No. 159*f*.
    g. *Heber Sale*, see Nos. 19*b*, 32*a*, 35*i*, 35*j*, 37*f*, 38*a*, 52*c*, 66*a*, 84*a*, 157*d*.
    h. *Hibbert Sale*, see Nos. 19*c*, 36*b*, 37*g*, 72*h*, 91*d*, 125*a*, 159*g*, 159*h*.
    i. *John Radcliffe's Libr.*, see No. 178*c*.
    j. *Kloss Sale*, see Nos. 4*a*, 5*a*, 9*b*, 10*a*.
    k. *Libri Sale*, see No. 19*d*.
    l. *Payne and Foss Cat.*, see No. 99*a*.
    m. *Pinelli Sale*, see Nos. 19*e*, 37*h*, 72*i*, 165*d*.
    n. *South Kensington Museum*, see No. 74*a*.

o. Stanley Sale, see No. 35*k*.

p. Sunderland Sale, see Nos. 158*a*, 165*e*.

q. Sykes Sale, see Nos. 8*a*, 35*l*.

r. Thorold Sale, see Nos. 8*b*, 35*m*, 37*i*, 52*d*, 140*b*,
165*f*.

s. Unspecified Sale, see No. 72*j*.

28. **Maëstricht**:

   a. Bibliotheek, see No. 71*d*.

29. **Manchester**:

   a. Mrs. Rylands' Libr., see Nos. 17*d*, 37*j*, 165*g*.

30. **Milano**:

   a. Bibl. Ambrosiana, see Nos. 105*a*, 164*b*.

   b. Bibl. Nazionale di Brera, see Nos. 105*b*, 105*c*,
151*a*, 164*c*, 164*d*.

31. **München**:

   a. Kgl. Hof- u. Stadtbibl., see Nos. 17*e*, 39*d*, 63*b*,
95*b*, 96*c*, 102*c*, 127*d*, 127*e*, 132*a*, 138*c*, 138*d*,
138*e*, 138*f*, 160*c*, 160*d*.

32. **Nevers**:

   a. Bibl. Municipale, see No. 136*a*.

33. **Nürnberg**:

   a. Stadtbibl., see No. 95*c*.

34. **Oxford**:

   a. Bodleian Libr., see Nos. 17*f*, 37*k*, 37*l*, 70*b*, 72*k*,
78*e*, 78*f*, 78*g*, 85*b*, 91*e*, 102*d*, 103*b*, 127*f*, 134*b*,
142*a*, 157*e*, 159*i*, 160*e*, 165*h*, 168*a*.

35. **Padova**:

   a. R. Bibl. Universitaria, see Nos. 127*g*, 164*e*.

36. **Paris**:

   a. Andry Sale, see No. 10*b*.

   b. Bearzi Sale, see Nos. 66*b*, 84*b*.

   c. Bibl. Nationale, see Nos. 9*c*, 20*a*, 40*a*, 41*a*, 51*b*,
54*b*, 58*c*, 59*b*, 61*b*, 67*a*, 112*b*, 143*d*, 156*a*.

   d. Bibl. de Sainte-Geneviève, see No. 143*c*.

   e. Boutourlin Sale, see Nos. 21*b*, 23*a*, 25*e*, 37*m*, 72*l*.

   f. Brienne-Laire Sale, see Nos. 11*d*, 14*a*, 38*b*, 52*e*,
72*m*, 106*a*, 165*i*.

g. Cailhava Sale, see No. 82*b*.

h. Celotti Sale, see No. 77*a*.

i. Costabili Sale, see No. 161*b*.

j. Coulon Sale, see No. 172*b*.

k. Du Fay Sale, see No. 62*a*.

l. Elcy Sale, see No. 16*a*.

m. Gaignat Sale, see No. 35*n*.

n. Golowkin Sale, see No. 12*c*.

o. Hervieux' Libr., see Nos. 10*c*, 119*a*, 141*b*.

p. La Vallière Sale, see Nos. 37*n*, 51*c*, 112*c*.

q. Libri Sale, see Nos. 37*o*, 72*n*, 85*c*.

r. MacCarthy Sale, see Nos. 9*d*, 10*d*, 35*o*, 37*p*.

s. Molini Sale, see Nos. 23*b*, 25*f*, 49*a*.

t. Morante Sale, see No. 10*e*.

u. Regnault-Bretel Sale, see No. 122*c*.

v. Reine Sale, see No. 159*j*.

w. Salle Silvestre, see Nos. 31*b*, 51*d*, 177*b*.

x. Soubise Sale, see No. 10*f*.

y. Unspecified Sale, see Nos. 44*a*, 72*o*, 82*c*, 139*c*, 157*f*.

z. Yéméniz Sale, see Nos. 7*b*, 52*f*, 54*c*.

37. **Prag**:
   a. Strahöfer Bibl., see No. 90*a*.

38. **Rio de Janeiro**:
   a. Bibl. Nacional, see No. 29*a*.

39. **Rome**:
   a. Unspecified Sale, see No. 21*c*.

40. **Rouen**:
   a. Bibl. Municipale, see No. 123*b*.

41. **Sevilla**:
   a. Bibl. Colombina, see Nos. 85*d*, 132*b*.

42. **St. Gallen**:
   a. Vadianische Bibl., see Nos. 66*c*, 96*d*, 140*c*.

43. **Stuttgart**:
   a. Kgl. Öffentliche Bibl., see Nos. 15*a*, 39*e*, 64*c*, 102*e*, 103*c*, 160*f*.

44. **Toulouse :**
    a. Bibl. du Collège, see Nos. 45*a*, 46*a*.
45. **Tours :**
    a. Bibl. Municipale, see No. 34*a*.
46. **Unknown :**
    a. See Nos. 13*a*, 18*a*, 22*a*, 26*a*, 27*a*, 28*a*, 32*b*, 35*p*,
        38*d*, 40*b*, 42*a*, 43*a*, 48*a*, 55*a*, 56*a*, 61*b* n, 65*a*,
        67*a* n, 68*a*, 69*a*, 72*q*, 73*a*, 79*a*, 83*a*, 87*a*, 88*a*,
        89*a*, 92*a*, 94*a*, 98*a* n, 100*a*, 104*a*, 108*a*, 110*a*,
        116*a*, 118*a*, 120*a*, 144*a*, 145*a*, 153*a*, 155*a*,
        156*a* n, 162*a*, 163*a*, 166*a*, 170*c*, 173*a*, 176*a*.
47. **Venezia :**
    a. Apostolo Zeno's Libr., see No. 50*a*.
    *b. Bibl. Monasterii S. Michaelis Venetiarum Prope
        Murianum,* see Nos. 140*d*, 141*c*.
    c. Bibl. Nazionale Marciana, see Nos. 47*a*, 117*b*,
        124*a*.
48. **Verona :**
    a. Bibl. Comunale, see Nos. 131*b*, 161*c*.
49. **Washington :**
    a. Libr. of Congress, see Nos. 37*q*, 140*e*.
50. **Wien :**
    a. Bibl. Albertina, see No. 38*c*.
    b. K. u. K. Hofbibl., see Nos. 17*g*, 39*f*, 44*b*, 47*b*, 72*p*,
        80*d*, 81*a*, 95*d*, 96*e*, 97*a*, 102*f*, 117*c*, 124*b*, 127*h*,
        160*g*.
51. **Windsor Castle :**
    a. Royal Libr., see Nos. 58*d*, 70*c*.
52. **Wolfenbüttel :**
    a. Herzogliche Bibl., see Nos. 1*a*, 17*h*, 127*i*.
53. **Würzburg :**
    a. Universitätsbibl., see Nos. 33*b*, 101*b*.

    h.   Alphabetical List of Sales and Catalogues.

1. **Andry Sale,** Paris, 1830, see No. 10*b*.
2. **Bearzi Sale,** Paris, 1855, see Nos. 66*b*, 84*b*.

3. **Beckford Sale,** London, 1882, see Nos. 35*c*, 117*a*, 131*a*.
4. **Bernard Quaritch Cat.,** London, 1874, see Nos. 17*c*, 72*e*.
5. **Bernard Quaritch Cat.,** London, 1886, see Nos. 7*a*, 35*d*, 35*e*, 35*f*, 53*b*. 169*a*.
6. **Bernard Quaritch Cat.,** London, 1888, see p. 29n and Nos. 112*a*, 133*a*.
7. **Bernard Quaritch Cat.,** London, 1894, see No. 25*a*.
8. **Bibliotheca Nacional,** Rio de Janeiro, 1885, see No. 29*a*.
9. **Bodleian Libr.,** Oxford, 1843, see Nos. 37*k*, 37*l*, 70*b*, 103*b*, 134*b*, 159*i*, 165*h*.
10. **Boston Public Libr.,** Boston, 1866, see Nos. 9*a*, 12*a*, 12*b*.
11. **Boutourlin Sale,** Paris, 1839-1841, see Nos. 21*b*, 23*a*, 25*e*, 37*m*, 72*l*.
12. **Brienne-Laire Sale,** Paris, 1791, see Nos. 11*d*, 14*a*, 38*b*, 52*e*, 72*m*, 106*a*, 165*i*.
13. **British Museum Catalogue of Printed Books,** London, 1883-1890, see p. 9n and Nos. 3*c*, 6*a*, 11*a*, 11*b*, 11*c*, 19*a*, 21*a*, 24*a*, 25*b*, 25*c*, 25*d*, 30*a*, 31*a*, 35*g*, 35*h*, 37*b*, 37*c*, 37*d*, 39*c*, 51*a*, 52*a*, 52*b*, 57*a*, 58*a*, 58*b*, 60*a*, 60*b*, 60*c*, 61*a*, 63*a*, 70*a*, 71*b*, 71*c*, 72*f*, 72*g*, 76*a*, 76*b*, 78*d*, 80*c*, 82*a*, 85*a*, 86*a*, 91*c*, 93*a*, 95*a*, 96*b*, 102*b*, 103*a*, 111*a*, 114*a*, 115*a*, 122*b*, 123*a*, 127*b*, 127*c*, 129*a*, 130*a*, 130*b*, 134*a*, 135*b*, 138*b*, 140*a*, 141*a*, 143*a*, 143*b*, 146*a*, 147*a*, 148*a*, 149*a*, 150*a*, 157*c*, 159*c*, 159*d*, 159*e*, 160*b*, 161*a*, 164*a*, 165*b*, 165*c*, 170*b*, 172*a*, 178*a*, 178*b*.
14. **Cailhava Sale,** Paris, 1845-1852, see No. 82*b*.
15. **Cassano Serra Sale,** London, (?), see No. 36*c*.
16. **Caxton Celebration,** London, 1877, see No. 37*a*.
17. **Celotti Sale,** Paris, 1825, see No. 77*a*.
18. **Costabili Sale,** Paris, (?), see No. 161*b*.
19. **Coulon Sale,** Paris, 1829, see No. 172*b*.
20. **Crevenna Sale,** Amsterdam, 1789, see Nos. 72*a*, 159*a*.

21. **Du Fay Sale**, Paris, 1725, see No. 62*a*.
22. **Elcy Sale**, Paris, (?), see No. 16*a*.
23. **Enschedé Sale**, Amsterdam, (?), see No. 3*a*.
24. **Gaignat Sale**, Paris, 1769, see No. 35*n*.
25. **Gennadius Sale**, London, 1895, see No. 159*f*.
26. **Golowkin Sale**, Paris, (?), see No. 12*c*.
27. **Grossherzogl. Hofbibl.**, Darmstadt, 1871, see Nos. 35*b*, 59*a*, 75*a*, 113*a*, 122*a*, 177*a*.
28. **Grossherzogl. Hof- und Landesbibl.**, Carlsruhe, 1877, see p. 28n and Nos. 121*a*, 174*a*.
29. **Heber Sale**, London, 1834–1836, see Nos. 19*b*, 32*a*, 35*i*, 35*j*, 37*f*, 38*a*, 52*c*, 66*a*, 84*a*, 157*d*.
30. **Hibbert Sale**, London, 1829, see Nos. 19*c*, 36*b*, 37*g*, 72*h*, 91*d*, 125*a*, 159*g*, 159*h*.
31. **Kloss Sale**, London, 1835, see Nos. 4*a*, 5*a*, 9*b*, 10*a*.
32. **La Vallière Sale**, Paris, 1767, see Nos. 37*n*, 51*c*, 112*c*.
33. **Library of Congress**, Washington, 1867, see No. 140*c*.
34. **Library of Congress**, Washington, 1878, see No. 37*q*.
35. **Libri Sale**, Paris, 1847–1858, see Nos. 37*o*, 72*n*, 85*c*.
36. **Libri Sale**, London, 1859, see No. 19*d*.
37. **MacCarthy Sale**, Paris, 1779, see Nos. 9*d*, 10*d*, 35*o*, 37*p*.
38. **Martinus Nijhoff Cat.**, The Hague, 1893, see No. 53*a*.
39. **Meermann Sale**, Amsterdam, (?), see Nos. 35*a*, 91*a*, 159*b*.
40. **Molini Sale**, Paris, 1813, see Nos. 23*b*, 25*f*, 49*a*.
41. **Monasterium S. Michaelis**, Venetiis, 1779, see Nòs. 140*d*, 141*c*.
42. **Morante Sale**, Paris, (?), see No. 10*e*.
43. **Payne and Foss Cat.**, London, 1824, see No. 99*a*.
44. **Pinelli Sale**, London, 1789, see Nos. 19*e*, 37*h*, 72*i*, 165*d*.

45. **Regnault-Bretel Sale**, Paris, 1819, see No. 122*c*.
46. **Reine Sale**, Paris, 1834–1840, see No. 159*j*.
47. **Salle Silvestre**, Paris, 1809, see Nos. 31*b*, 51*d*, 177*b*.
48. **Soubise Sale**, Paris, 1788, see No. 10*f*.
49. **Stanley Sale**, London, (?), see No. 35*k*.
50. **Strong Sale**, New York, 1878, see No. 64*a*.
51. **Sunderland Sale**, London, 1881, see Nos. 158*a*, 165*e*.
52. **Sykes Sale**, London, 1824, see Nos. 8*a*, 35*l*.
53. **Thorold Sale**, London, 1884, see Nos. 8*b*, 35*m*, 37*i*, 52*d*, 140*b*, 165*f*.
54. **Unspecified Sale**, Rome, 1478, see No. 21*c*.
55. **Unspecified Sale**, London, 1816, see No. 72*j*.
56. **Unspecified Sale**, Paris, 1856, see No. 44*a*.
57. **Unspecified Sale**, Paris, (?), see Nos. 72*o*, 82*c*, 139*c*, 157*f*.
58. **Vadianische Bibl.**, St. Gallen, 1864, see Nos. 66*c*, 96*d*, 140*c*.
59. **Yéméniz Sale**, Paris, 1868, see Nos. 7*b*, 52*f*, 54*c*.

i. Chronological List of Sales and Catalogues.

1. **1478, Unspecified Sale**, Rome, see No. 21*c*.
2. **1725, Du Fay Sale**, Paris, see No. 62*a*.
3. **1767, La Vallière Sale**, Paris, see Nos. 37*n*, 51*c*, 112*c*.
4. **1769, Gaignat Sale**, Paris, see No. 35*n*.
5. **1779, MacCarthy Sale**, Paris, see Nos. 9*d*, 10*d*, 35*o*, 37*p*.
6. **1779, Monasterium S. Michaelis**, Venetiis, see No. 140*d*.
7. **1788, Soubise Sale**, Paris, see No. 10*f*.
8. **1789, Crevenna Sale**, Amsterdam, see Nos. 72*a*, 159*a*.
9. **1789, Pinelli Sale**, London, see Nos. 19*e*, 37*h*, 72*i*, 165*d*.
10. **1791, Brienne-Laire Sale**, Paris, see Nos. 11*d*, 14*a*, 38*b*, 52*e*, 72*m*, 106*a*, 165*i*.

11. **1809, Salle Silvestre,** Paris, see Nos. 31*b*, 51*d*, 177*b*.
12. **1813, Molini Sale,** Paris, see Nos. 23*b*, 25*f*, 49*a*.
13. **1816, Unspecified Sale,** London, see No. 72*j*.
14. **1819, Regnault-Bretel Sale,** Paris, see No. 122*c*.
15. **1824, Payne and Foss Cat.,** London, see No. 99*a*.
16. **1824, Sykes Sale,** London, see Nos. 8*a*, 35*l*.
17. **1825, Celotti Sale,** Paris, see No. 77*a*.
18. **1829, Coulon Sale,** Paris, see No. 172*b*.
19. **1829, Hibbert Sale,** London, see Nos. 19*c*, 36*b*, 37*g*, 72*h*, 91*d*, 125*a*, 159*g*, 159*h*.
20. **1830, Andry Sale,** Paris, see No. 10*b*.
21. **1834-1836, Heber Sale,** London, see Nos. 19*b*, 32*a*, 35*i*, 35*j*, 37*f*, 38*a*, 52*c*, 66*a*, 84*a*, 157*d*.
22. **1834-1840, Reine Sale,** Paris, see No. 159*j*.
23. **1835, Kloss Sale,** London, see Nos. 4*a*, 5*a*, 9*b*, 10*a*.
24. **1839-1841, Boutourlin Sale,** Paris, see Nos. 21*b*, 23*a*, 25*c*, 37*m*, 72*l*.
25. **1843, Bodleian Libr.,** Oxford, see Nos. 37*k*, 37*l*, 70*b*, 103*b*, 134*b*, 159*i*, 165*h*.
26. **1845-1852, Cailhava Sale,** Paris, see No. 82*b*.
27. **1847-1858, Libri Sale,** Paris, see Nos. 37*o*, 72*n*, 85*c*.
28. **1855, Bearzi Sale,** Paris, see Nos. 66*b*, 84*b*.
29. **1856, Unspecified Sale,** Paris, see No. 44*a*.
30. **1859, Libri Sale,** London, see No. 19*d*.
31. **1864, Vadianische Bibl.,** St. Gallen, see Nos. 66*c*, 96*d*, 140*c*.
32. **1866, Boston Public Libr.,** Boston, see Nos. 9*a*, 12*a*, 12*b*.
33. **1867, Library of Congress,** Washington, see No. 140*e*.
34. **1868, Yéméniz Sale,** Paris, see Nos. 7*b*, 52*f*, 54*c*.
35. **1871, Grossherzogl. Hofbibl.,** Darmstadt, see Nos. 35*b*, 59*a*, 75*a*, 113*a*, 122*a*, 177*a*.
36. **1874, Bernard Quaritch Cat.,** London, see Nos. 17*c*, 72*e*.

37. **1877, Caxton Celebration,** London, see No. 37*a*.
38. **1877, Grossherzogl. Hof- und Landesbibl.,** Carlsruhe, see p. 28n and Nos. 121*a*, 174*a*.
39. **1878, Library of Congress,** Washington, see No. 37*q*.
40. **1878, Strong Sale,** New York, see No. 64*a*.
41. **1881, Sunderland Sale,** London, see Nos. 158*a*, 165*e*.
42. **1882, Beckford Sale,** London, see Nos. 35*c*, 117*a*, 131*a*.
43. **1883–1890, British Museum Catalogue of Printed Books,** London, see p. 9n, and Nos. 3*c*, 6*a*, 11*a*, 11*b*, 11*c*, 19*a*, 21*a*, 24*a*, 25*b*, 25*c*, 25*d*, 30*a*, 31*a*, 35*g*, 35*h*, 37*b*, 37*c*, 37*d*, 39*c*, 51*a*, 52*a*, 52*b*, 57*a*, 58*a*, 58*b*, 60*a*, 60*b*, 60*c*, 61*a*, 63*a*, 70*a*, 71*b*, 71*c*, 72*f*, 72*g*, 76*a*, 76*b*, 78*d*, 80*c*, 82*a*, 85*a*, 86*a*, 91*c*, 93*a*, 95*a*, 96*b*, 102*b*, 103*a*, 111*a*, 114*a*, 115*a*, 122*b*, 123*a*, 127*b*, 127*c*, 129*a*, 130*a*, 130*b*, 134*a*, 135*b*, 138*b*, 140*a*, 141*a*, 143*a*, 143*b*, 146*a*, 147*a*, 148*a*, 149*a*, 150*a*, 157*c*, 159*c*, 159*d*, 159*e*, 160*b*, 161*a*, 164*a*, 165*b*, 165*c*, 170*b*, 172*a*, 178*a*, 178*b*.
44. **1884, Thorold Sale,** London, see Nos. 8*b*, 35*m*, 37*i*, 52*d*, 140*b*, 165*f*.
45. **1885, Bibliotheca Nacional,** Rio de Janeiro, see No. 29*a*.
46. **1886, Bernard Quaritch Cat.,** London, see Nos. 7*a*, 35*d*, 35*e*, 35*f*, 53*b*, 169*a*.
47. **1888, Bernard Quaritch Cat.,** London, see p. 29n and Nos. 112*a*, 133*a*.
48. **1893, Martinus Nijhoff Cat.,** The Hague, see No. 53*a*.
49. **1894, Bernard Quaritch Cat.,** London, see No. 25*a*.
50. **1895, Gennadius Sale,** London, see No. 159*f*.
51. **?   Cassano Serra Sale,** London, see No. 36*c*.

52. ? **Costabili Sale,** Paris, see No. 161*b*.
53. ? **Elcy Sale,** Paris, see No. 16*a*.
54. ? **Enschedé Sale,** Amsterdam, see No. 3*a*.
55. ? **Golowkin Sale,** Paris, see No. 12*c*.
56. ? **Meermann Sale,** Amsterdam, see Nos. 35*a*,
        91*a*, 159*b*.
57. ? **Morante Sale,** Paris, see No. 10*e*.
58. ? **Stanley Sale,** London, see No. 35*k*.
59. ? **Unspecified Sale,** Paris, see Nos. 72*o*, 82*c*,
        139*c*, 157*f*.

j. Prices Brought.

A. London Sales.

1. **12s. 6d.**, see No. 19*e*.
2. **£1 1s.**, see No. 19*b*.
3. **£1 13s.**, see Nos. 66*a*, 84*a*.
4. **£1 16s.**, see No. 52*c*.
5. **£2 5s.**, see No. 91*d*.
6. **£2 12s.**, see No. 19*d*.
7. **£2 19s.**, see No. 157*d*.
8. **£3**, see No. 32*a*.
9. **£3 7s.**, see No. 35*i*.
10. **£3 13s.**, see No. 159*g*.
11. **£3 14s.**, see No. 35*j*.
12. **£3 15s.**, see No. 159*h*.
13. **£4 1s.**, see No. 38*a*.
14. **£4 4s.**, see No. 125*a*.
15. **£5**, see No. 169*a*.
16. **£6**, see No. 37*f*.
17. **£6 16s. 6d.**, see No. 36*b*.
18. **£7 10s.**, see No. 53*b*.
19. **£8 18s. 6d.**, see No. 35*l*.
20. **£9 5s.**, see No. 37*g*.
21. **£12**, see No. 72*i*.
22. **£12 15s.**, see No. 19*c*.

23. **£14**, see No. 37*h*.
24. **£14 3s. 6d.**, see No. 8*a*.
25. **£15**, see No. 17*c*.
26. **£17**, see No. 72*h*.
27. **£20**, see Nos. 35*d*, 112*a*.
28. **£26 15s.**, see No. 72*j*.
29. **£31 10s.**, see No. 80*b*n.
30. **£40**, see No. 35*e*.
31. **£40 19s.**, see No. 165*d*.
32. **£42**, see No. 35*k*.
33. **£50**, see No. 25*a*.
34. **£63**, see No. 35*f*.
35. **£80**, see No. 72*e*.
36. **£100**, see No. 7*a*.
37. **£250**, see No. 133*a*.
38. **£320**, see No. 133*a*n.

B. Paris Sales.

1. **3fr.**, see No. 21*c*.
2. **12fr.**, see No. 112*c*.
3. **14fr.**, see No. 52*e*.
4. **18fr.**, see No. 122*c*.
5. **21fr.**, see No. 177*b*.
6. **25fr.**, see Nos. 31*b*, 139*c*.
7. **27fr.**, see No. 14*a*.
8. **30fr.**, see Nos. 11*d*, 38*b*.
9. **36fr. 50c.**, see No. 72*l*.
10. **40fr. 50c.**, see Nos. 23*a*, 25*e*.
11. **41fr.**, see No. 159*j*.
12. **42fr.**, see No. 106*a*.
13. **45fr.**, see No. 161*b*.
14. **81fr.**, see No. 77*a*.
15. **87fr.**, see No. 51*c*.
16. **88fr.**, see No. 35*o*.
17. **96fr.**, see No. 35*u*.
18. **100fr.**, see No. 10*f*.

19. **121fr.**, see No. 37*n*.
20. **134fr.**, see No. 51*d*.
21. **170fr.**, see No. 157*f*.
22. **175fr.**, see Nos. 85*c*, 172*b*.
23. **180fr.**, see No. 44*a*.
24. **185fr.**, see No. 37*m*.
25. **190fr.**, see Nos. 66*b*, 84*b*.
26. **199fr.**, see No. 82*b*.
27. **200fr.**, see No. 165*i*.
28. **205fr.**, see No. 10*e*.
29. **220fr.**, see Nos. 23*b*, 25*f*.
30. **250fr.**, see No. 37*o*.
31. **299fr.**, see No. 10*b*.
32. **400fr.**, see Nos. 37*p*, 52*f*.
33. **480fr.**, see No. 72*n*.
34. **606fr.**, see No. 72*m*.
35. **650fr.**, see No. 82*c*.
36. **685fr.**, see Nos. 9*d*, 10*d*.
37. **700fr.**, see Nos. 9*d*n, 10*d*n.
38. **1100fr.**, see No. 7*b*.
39. **1610fr.**, see No. 72*o*.
40. **2000fr.**, see No. 54*c*n.
41. **3000fr.**, see No. 2*a*n.
42. **6000fr.**, see No. 54*c*.

C. Amsterdam Sales.

1. **25fl.**, see No. 159*a*.
2. **30fl.**, see No. 91*a*.
3. **41fl.**, see No. 159*b*.
4. **50fl.**, see Nos. 35*a*, 53*a*.
5. **180fl.**, see No. 72*a*.
6. **400fl.**, see No. 3*a*.

D. Florence Sales.

1. **168l.**, see No. 49*a*.

E. New York Sales.

1. **$17.50**, see No. 64*a*.

k. Bibliographers' Vidimus.*

1. **Amador de los Rios** has seen No. 98*a*.
2. **Brunet** has seen Nos. 1*a*, 2*a*, 67*a*.
3. **Deschamps** (or **G. Brunet**) has seen No. 9*c*.
4. **Ghivizzani** has seen No. 36*a*.
5. **Hervieux** has seen Nos. 15*a*, 17*b*, 17*c*, 17*f*, 17*g*, 25*c*, 25*d*, 30*a*, 33*b*, 38*c*, 39*a*, 39*c*, 39*d*, 39*e*, 44*b*, 47*a*, 47*b*, 57*a*, 58*a*, 61*b*, 63*a*, 63*b*, 64*b*, 64*c*, 70*a*, 70*b*, 71*a*, 71*b*, 71*c*, 71*d*, 74*a*, 78*a*, 78*b*, 78*c*, 78*d*, 78*e*, 78*f*, 78*g*, 80*a*, 80*b*, 81*a*, 98*a*, 101*b*, 105*a*, 105*b*, 105*c*, 117*b*, 117*c*, 124*a*, 124*b*, 143*d*, 151*a*.
6. **Keidel, G. C.**, has seen No. 64*a*.
7. **Morel-Fatio** has seen No. 156*a*.
8. **Morelli** has seen No. 50*a*.
9. **Robert** has seen Nos. 32*b*, 35*p*, 38*d*, 40*b*, 61*b*, 67*a*, 72*q*, 144*a*, 156*a*, 170*c*, 173*a*.
10. **Schwabe** has seen No. 17*h*.

l. Former Owners.†

1. **Benard, Pieri**, see No. 2*a*n.
2. **Colombo, Ferdinando**, see No. 85*d*n.
3. **Cracherode, C. M.**, see No. 37*c*n.
4. **Grolierus, Io.**, see No. 133*a*n.
5. **Ireland, Thomas**, see No. 35*e*n.
6. **Kirkbye, Bartholomew**, see No. 35*e*n.
7. **Lakelands**, see No. 159*f*n.
8. **Leslie**, see No. 19*d*n.
9. **McCoy, John W.**, see No. 64*a*n.

---

* The great majority of the catalogues and bibliographies consulted by me were as a rule so indefinite in their statements that I have been able to include only a few references in this list; to do otherwise would have been giving the semblance of fact to only the merest conjectures for most of the copies not mentioned in this short list.

† This list includes only those names which have not been given in the lists of Sales and Catalogues because of a lack of the necessary information.

10. **Préfond, Girardot de,** see No. 112*an.*
11. **Stokesley, Nicholas,** see No. 35*en.*
12. **Thacker, Robert,** see No. 35*en.*
13. **Walker, Fountaine,** see No. 25*an.*
14. **Yéméniz,** see No. 72*en.*

www.ingramcontent.com/pod-product-compliance
Lightning Source LLC
Chambersburg PA
CBHW030545270326
41927CB00008B/1513